FOUR
FUNERALS
and a
WEDDING

Also by Jill Smolowe

A Love Like No Other: Stories from Adoptive Parents (co-editor)

An Empty Lap: One Couple's Journey to Parenthood

FOUR FUNERALS
and a
WEDDING

Resilience in a Time of Grief

JILL SMOLOWE

SHE WRITES PRESS

Brief excerpts from this book appeared in different form in *The Washington Post Magazine* and *More.*

Published 2014
Printed in the United States of America
ISBN: 978-1-938314-72-8
Library of Congress Control Number: 2013953914

For information, address:
She Writes Press
1563 Solano Ave #546
Berkeley, CA 94707

In Memory of:

Joe Treen, my husband
Ann Smolowe, my sister
Greta Smolowe, my mother
Esmeralda Treen, my mother-in-law

CONTENTS

Prologue 1

1 Diagnosis. 11

2 Road Map 27

3 Surrender. 43

4 Rorschach Blot 61

5 Lifelines. 79

6 Contagion 101

7 Death 121

8 Preconceptions. 139

9 Gratitude. 155

10 Serendipity. 173

11 Solace 193

12 Commemoration. 213

Epilogue. 231

Postscript. 241

PROLOGUE

FUNNY, THE MOMENTS THAT STICK IN MEMORY. I have one that I can't pinpoint more precisely than a morning in the early 2000s, yet I remember it like yesterday. I've just pulled into the parking lot of a small shopping center near my home in Montclair, New Jersey. As I step out of the car I spot Elizabeth, the wife of a journalist with whom my husband and I worked two decades earlier. Though I barely know Elizabeth, I know an intimate detail about her life: her husband Jake is battling a deadly blood cancer.

I don't recall how or when my husband and I first learned about Jake's illness, but I do remember our shock and concern. I also remember our hesitation. By the time news of the cancer reached us, Jake was already months into treatment and facing a stem cell transplant. Was it too late to acknowledge his illness? After much discussion, we decided to send a note. Joe promptly punted. "You're better at this sort of thing," he said, giving new meaning to our mutual nickname for each other: Weasel. After several drafts, I settled on a message that struck a note of humor (not too grim) and breezily offered help with carpools and dinners (not too pushy). Joe and I signed the card, one of us posted it, time passed. It might have been a few months; it might have been many.

What I do remember sharply, clearly—a short film that I can see in my mind's eye—is this next sequence in the parking lot. I get out of my Subaru, see Elizabeth, and freeze. Her head is tilted toward the ground and her shoulders are rounded, as if bearing too heavy a load. Her slow gait radiates exhaustion, as if the act of putting one foot in front of the other requires effort. The sight of her chills me. Plainly, this is a woman sunk in a hell I can't imagine.

Yet I do plenty of imagining as I watch Elizabeth make her way across the lot. Latching on to those aspects of her life that are similar to mine—wife, mother, working woman, Montclair resident—I project what worries must be weighting her every step. *Her husband might die...Her children might lose their father...Family finances might become a wreck...They might have to relocate...*The jumble of emotions that accompany my thoughts are impossible to untangle. Sympathy? Concern? Pity? Fear? Horror? One thing I don't feel: empathy. Unlike Elizabeth, I have never been at risk of losing my husband.

Move! yells a voice in my head. *Say something to her!*

Leave her alone! another voice counters.

Paralyzed by indecision, I debate. Maybe I should approach Elizabeth and ask how Jake is doing. Give her a supportive hug. Offer to assist with her errands. Then again, it might be more considerate to leave her undisturbed. It's a school day. Perhaps this is a rare opportunity for Elizabeth to be alone with her fears and worries. Besides, she might not recognize me; we've met only a few times. How awkward would *that* be, some stranger gushing commiseration in her face? Yet inaction feels cowardly. And wouldn't a failure to acknowledge the monumental changes in Elizabeth's life fall short of some basic standard of compassion? Because it doesn't occur to me that Elizabeth might be thinking of anything but the upsetting events in her life, it doesn't occur to me simply to shout hello and wave. No, her situation is all consuming; her distress requires a sensitive response. But which is the right one?

As I deliberate, Elizabeth crosses the street and disappears into a store. I am left standing by my car, feeling like a chicken so feckless that I can't even get it together to cross the street.

Here's another moment embedded in memory, only this one I can pinpoint precisely: January 3, 2007. I am at the same small shopping center in Montclair, this time running errands in preparation to drive my husband into Manhattan for his 1:00 p.m. check-in at St. Luke's-Roosevelt Hospital. Not quite two days have passed since we learned by phone the cause of Joe's recent fatigue: a deadly blood cancer. Already, that call feels like it came a lifetime ago.

Now that we've made the many arrangements that will enable Joe to disappear from his life for the next five months—or maybe forever—my husband is sinking deeper into himself. I, conversely, am turned outward, a tuning fork calibrated to both Joe's emotional needs and the practical aspects of getting him ready for his first four-week hospital stay. The shock of Weasel's diagnosis has left me with an uncanny clarity about what I stand to lose and what role I must play to maximize his chances of recovery.

My errands complete, I stand at a curb waiting to cross the street. I monitor the cars coming from my left, turn to watch the traffic flowing from the right, then look straight ahead. At the same moment that my gaze lands on the parking lot, I remember Elizabeth and hear these words, shrill, in my head: "Oh, my God, I am now *that woman.*"

In a rush, the meaning of those two words hits me with unsparing clarity. *That Woman.* The one who confuses instincts and makes people's tongues stick to the roofs of their mouths: What to do? What to say? *That Woman.* The one who triggers a confusion of concern and sympathy, fear and unease. The one who makes people wonder, Could it happen to me? Could I cope? The woman who reminds them that a spouse can get sick. That children can lose their parents. That plans, expectations, and dreams can evaporate. *That Woman.* The one, to put it bluntly, who you are very, very grateful you are not.

For two days now, I've been focused on the three most obvious threats to my existence: I'm at risk of losing my husband; our twelve-year-old daughter, Becky, is at risk of losing her father; all three of us are at risk of losing the wonderful life we've built together. Now, I detect yet another threat. In the rush of sympathy that makes people say too much or too little or, like me, nothing at all; in the crush of pity that leaves no room for laughter or casual chitchat; in the tide of anxious questions that drowns out conversation about books, parenting, lousy commutes, or anything else that reminds large parts of my life remain intact, I am at risk of losing my strength, my optimism, my interest in the world outside my head. I am at risk of losing the person Joe and Becky are counting on to hold their lives steady during the long battle ahead. In short, I am at risk of losing me.

No! my mind screams. *Move!*

I step off the curb and cross the street, determined to handle whatever lies on the other side.

What waited on the other side was a tempest of startling proportion. The chemo treatments that quarantined Joe for the better part of five months, followed by the stem cell transplant that isolated him for two months more, would prove mere warning squalls. For the next three years, shock bulletins, hospitalizations, and grim prognoses battered my world relentlessly.

A few more dates seared in my memory:

March 28, 2009: My mother-in-law dies.

June 20, 2009: My husband dies.

August 14, 2010: My sister dies.

September 1, 2010: My mother dies.

I know. Unimaginable. In less than a year and a half, I lost not only the man who was the center of my life, but also three of the women who gave it shape and meaning. I kept anticipating that the accumulating weight of so much sorrow would sink me into depression and despair, bringing my life and thoughts to a standstill. Dark logic reasoned that so much of my world had shattered; surely I would, too. The pained winces and concerned questions of caring friends telegraphed a similar expectation. So did a lifetime of cultural cues absorbed through memoirs, films, novels, and TV shows, each wrenching portrait of loss reinforcing what I'd been taught is the definitive word on bereavement: Elisabeth Kübler-Ross's five-stage cycle of grief.

To my surprise and relief, my grief never cut me off or shut me down. As I put the finishing touches on this book three years after losing Joe, my strength, optimism, and interest in the world outside my head remain sturdy. That's not to say I don't still experience gusts of sorrow. I do, almost daily. But with heartache has come an unexpected sweetness that has cushioned, fortified, and ultimately renewed me. Friendships have deepened. Relationships with remaining family members have developed a new level of intimacy. The unthinkable loss of my husband has given rise to the unexpected joy of new love.

For me, all of this serendipity has exerted a counterbalancing force that has left me disinclined to deny, evade, or flee from my moments of intense pain. I know I can tolerate them because I know they will pass.

I also know that my way of processing and dealing with grief is just that: mine and mine alone. Informed by a combination of coping mechanisms, beliefs, and attitudes that crystallized during the two and a half years my husband was ill, I can be quite unsentimental (or maybe the word is stubborn) about doing it my way. Not long after Joe died, a yoga instructor asked me how I was doing. "Bereavement sucks big time," I said. Her shocked expression indicated this was not the way a loving widow was supposed to respond.

Which brings me to the focus of this book. Throughout the last five years, neither my needs nor my behavior have matched the American cultural script for exhausted caregivers, heartbroken widows, and grieving family members. I say "script" because the well-intentioned responses I've encountered all along the way—no matter how well or how little I know a person—have been largely uniform and seemingly predicated on assumptions similar to mine that long-ago day in the parking lot with Elizabeth. The thinking goes something like this: Jill's days must be an unrelieved stream of worry, anguish, and sorrow. Her life is so awful that she must be incapable of thinking or talking about anything else. Jill needs consolation and reassurance. The script then calls for dialogue about my fragile state of mind and disrupted life. (Stage directions: Interlocutor looks concerned. Jill looks stricken. After conversation, Jill looks soothed by the expression of caring and support.)

For me, that scenario never had its intended effect. From the start, the commiseration was more burdensome than helpful, a reaction that is hardly unique. Several fellow travelers—wives tending a seriously ill spouse; widows and widowers coping with bereavement; family members dealing with loss—have told me that they find the unremitting sympathy exhausting, frustrating, sometimes even maddening. By the time worst came to worst with Joe, I felt no inclination to seek solace in the pages of books that affirmed my feelings of devastation. Nor did I want to hear, as I frequently did, that I was "amazing" for bearing up so well. Statements like that made me feel my coping mechanisms and grief were abnormal. What I hungered for were accounts that shed light on and supported my determination to find my way back to a place where I could look forward to, rather than dread, getting out of bed in the morning.

Help arrived four months after Joe's death with the publication of George A. Bonanno's *The Other Side of Sadness: What the New Science of Bereavement Tells Us About Life After Loss.* "Humans are wired to survive," Bonanno, a clinical psychologist and leading expert on grief, wrote. "Resilience is the norm." Unlike Kübler-Ross, who relied on observations of her dying patients to formulate her theory, Bonanno methodically sought out bereaved populations to conduct his research. Over two decades, he identified three distinct patterns of bereavement, irrespective of the age of the mourner or the loss involved (spouse, child, parent, or sibling): *chronic grief* (the 10 to 15 percent who are overwhelmed by grief for eighteen months or longer); *acute grief* (the 15 to 20 percent who recover within eighteen months); and *resilience* (the more than 50 percent who return to normal functioning within six months). Those in the largest category, he found, experience grief as a constant oscillation between sadness and lighter moments that enable them not only to endure their sorrow, but also "to have genuinely pleasurable experiences, to laugh or indulge in moments of joy, even in the earliest days and weeks after loss."

What a relief. I wasn't amazing; my grief wasn't abnormal. Like most bereaved people, I was experiencing waves of sorrow interspersed with restorative thoughts, conversations, and activities that helped me to withstand, rather than be overwhelmed by, my pain. Bonanno's research also validated my sense of how people regarded me. "What is perhaps most intriguing about resilience is not how prevalent it is; rather it is that we are consistently surprised by it," he wrote. "We expect bereaved persons to feel constant sadness and grief. When they do not, we tend to be surprised."

Or judgmental. Ruth Davis Konigsberg, author of *The Truth About Grief*, a book that debunks Kübler-Ross's grief cycle and explores how the theory impedes resilience, has concluded that the five-stage theory is so dominant in our culture that it has "narrowed our emotional repertoire for loss, and stigmatizes reactions that diverge from its prescribed path."

With this memoir, I hope to expand that emotional repertoire by giving a voice to the silent majority whose instinctive response to death is resilience. Rather than surveying grief through the familiar lens of sorrow, I will focus on what has helped me—and what has not—to absorb, tolerate, and rebound from so much sickness and loss. To make sense of my "resilience," I will also explore the caregiving phase that preceded the deaths of my husband, sister, and mother. For me, and I suspect for many others who have seen loved ones through protracted and ultimately fatal disease, the coping mechanisms that evolved during the years of illness are inextricable from those that kicked in after hope gave way to bereavement. The caregiving and the grief, in other words, inform each other.

Here and there, I've relied on journal entries to provide unfiltered access to my thinking and feelings at critical moments. To safeguard privacy, I've used pseudonyms for all but my family members. While I have checked back with friends and relatives to freshen my memory of certain events, this account reflects my own recollections. Fault for any errors lies with me.

I realize that by training my lens on what has helped me cope, rather than what has made me (and still makes me) ache, I may be misperceived as a person who does not love or care deeply. It feels worth the risk. The outsized Baby Boom generation is now grappling with not only the intermittent caregiving challenges of middle-aged partners, but also the painful end-of-life decisions that often close out a parent's twilight years. Illness and grief are touching more and more lives. If I am able to offer anything that helps a caregiver, patient, or mourner get support that better meets his or her needs, then the effort feels very worthwhile to me.

Finally, I want to stress that by sharing my story, I aim only to enlarge assumptions about caregiving and grief, not to suggest that anybody else's experience will or should mirror mine. While loss is universal, grief is personal. Each journey is unique, the welter of thoughts and feelings individual and often cloudy. A person in profound pain can find it difficult to identify, let alone articulate, needs—particularly when the assumptions and concerns of loving friends and family are so relentlessly uniform that they bear the weight of expectation. Perhaps if we toss out the one-size-fits-all script and instead remain open to what a caregiver or person in mourning may actually be feeling, then those who are suffering will be better able to identify and communicate their needs—and those who want to ease that suffering will be better able to offer support that truly helps.

1

DIAGNOSIS

On the couch in my husband's home office, I sat clutching a throw pillow to my stomach as I listened to Joe's end of a phone conversation with his doctor. "Oh," he said. "Oh." I'd heard this litany countless times before, Joe's way of coaxing information from sources when reporting a story. Now, each new "oh" tightened my grip on the pillow. That his hematologist was going on at such length was disturbing. That Joe was taking so many notes was not reassuring. That Dr. B was speaking to him at 6:00 p.m. on New Year's Day, no, that could not be good at all. With his back to me, I couldn't see Joe's face, but his body language was eloquent, each monosyllable rounding his shoulders a bit more. At one point, he put his pen down and massaged his forehead.

Suddenly, Joe's voice rose. "Oh!" Grabbing the pen, he wrote furiously. "Is there a name for it?" His next "oh" was so quiet and flat that my skin prickled. *Take your time*, I thought. *No rush.*

I stopped listening and turned my attention to the walls and surfaces of Joe's office. This was not an act of denial; it was an expression of bizarre clarity. I was clear—very clear—that I was looking at relics from *before*. Once Joe named this "oh," I would be hurled into an *after* stripped of my comfortable assumptions about our life together. Nobody has ever accused me of patience, but as my eyes scanned Joe's artifacts, I felt no urgency to meet the woman I was about to become.

Over his standing desk, photos documented a journalism career that had taken Joe to Europe, the Middle East, Vietnam. Down the length of a window hung framed playbills from readings and stage productions of his full-length comedies, evidence of the humor and creativity that had drawn me to him back when we were both foreign affairs writers at *Newsweek*. On his computer desk, mounds of manila files and reporter's notebooks bespoke a work life still at full throttle. On the wood floor, gum wrappers, stray pens, dusty magazines, and yellowing newspapers demonstrated that even after twenty-four years of living with a neat freak, my Weasel (aka Wease) still resisted domestication.

Once upon a time, I'd put our relationship on the line with an ultimatum: marry me or move out. Long story short: He balked. I left. He proposed. Joe continued to protest right up to our wedding day, April 21, 1985. When I arrived at the altar of the UN chapel literally trembling, he circled my waist with his arm and held me until I was steady. That moment would prove an apt metaphor for our marriage, each of us a reliable ballast to the other's craziness. We agreed that only one of us could indulge our demons at any given time, and would break that rule only once, when I demanded during our eighth year of marriage that we finally start a family. Twelve months later we learned that we'd outlived our reproductive options. Joe thought the fireworks were over. Instead, I detonated a new explosion by insisting that we explore adoption. As we boarded a plane for China in January 1995, I wasn't certain that Joe would stick around after we returned with our new daughter. Long story short: We went. He saw. She conquered.

Joe's office clutter offered ample evidence that twelve years later he was still down for the count. "For Daddy from Becky" read the crayoned note taped to a door by his desk. "I [heart] you" read the note taped to a window shade over his fax machine. On the windowsill abutting his computer, he'd placed an array of framed photos: Becky. Me. Becky and me. Whether Joe was working, talking on the phone, or sneaking games of Free Cell, Becky and I were with him. In my own basement office, I had a similar photo assemblage on the ledge over my computer: Becky. Joe. Becky and Joe. Not a day went by that I didn't pause in my writing to look at those pictures and remind myself that the mainstays of my happiness were right in front of me.

"Really? That fast?" Joe's voice drew me back. "Tomorrow at ten is fine." Pause. "She can come, too? Good."

Joe hung up, then swiveled round in his chair and offered only one word: "Leukemia."

While we stared blankly at each other, my stomach took the express elevator to hell. My brain lagged a few seconds behind, pausing for an inappropriate reaction much like my shocked reaction while watching a live feed of the first World Trade Center tower crumbling: *Wait, that can't be right. Rewind! Do it again!*

Crossing the room, I perched on Joe's knee and wrapped my arms around him. His next words startled me almost as much as the diagnosis. "This is because of my arrogance." What? "It's because I assumed I'd live to a very old age, like my parents." What! Are you saying this is your fault? "I have a good wife, a good daughter, a good job, a good home. I should have known my luck wouldn't continue."

I pulled back to scrutinize Wease's expression. During our almost quarter century together, he'd never once shown a hint of fatalism. Where was the guy who years earlier had declined to sign a living will because he feared that I, a proponent of euthanasia, might pull the plug too soon? Where was the man who set large goals, then pursued them with such fierce determination, always finishing what he started, that we'd coined the word "completist" to describe him? I understood this was Joe's shock talking. But was it possible my tenacious husband was not going to wage the battle of his life? The very thought yielded a flash of clarity: *My turn to keep us grounded.*

Tightening my hug, I expressed my love. Expressed my wonder that while marriages were falling apart all around us, ours kept getting stronger. Expressed my confidence that Joe would fight this. Expressed my optimism that, given his amazing fitness at age sixty-four, he would be one of those who added to the survival statistics. Then I said, "What is leukemia exactly? I mean, I know it's hideous, but I don't know what it is. Do you?" When Joe shook his head, I pointed to his computer screen. "Let's Google it."

Okay, here we go. Leukemia, a cancer of the bone marrow and the blood. So, that explained the inconsistent results of several tests Joe had taken over the last six weeks, set in motion when a standard complete blood count, or CBC, returned mildly irregular results. When a second test again produced odd counts, Joe was referred to Dr. B, who told him with a smile, "Don't worry your pretty little head," then ordered blood tests three, four, and five, followed by a bone marrow biopsy. Though that last one jarred us (me a little, Joe a lot), by then we'd scouted the Internet and found nothing that matched his erratic blood counts.

As for Joe's complaints of fatigue, shortness of breath, and weakness, they came and they went between his twenty-mile bike rides through the mountains surrounding our weekend house in rural Pennsylvania. Moreover, that first CBC had been a mandatory precursor to arthroscopic surgery to mend Joe's right rotator cuff, which my buff husband had torn overdoing his weight workouts at the gym—hardly a recipe for some dread disease. So as the year-end holidays took us to Vermont for Thanksgiving with my sister's family, California for Christmas with Joe's family, then Pennsylvania for New Year's with our country friends, I let Joe do the worrying. Me? I figured he had a nasty cold or flu.

I pointed to Joe's computer screen. Does that say there are four kinds of leukemia? Which one did Dr. B say you have? She didn't say? "Call her back." From somewhere off in la-la-land, Joe said it could wait until tomorrow. "Call her back now," I said firmly. "We're not going to waste time researching the wrong disease."

Reluctantly, he dialed Dr. B's number. Again, she took his call. "You have acute myelogenous leukemia," she said. "If you have to have it, this is the best kind to have."

That lifted our mood sufficiently for me to suggest separate Internet searches so we could gather information more quickly. After agreeing to share the diagnosis with no one until after our consult with Dr. B, I headed downstairs to my office, thinking, *The best kind to have.* Then, I started to read. Acute myelogenous leukemia, an acute blood cancer, meaning one that comes on fast. No stage 1 to ease you into the idea. No stage 2 holding out hope that you'd caught it early enough. No stage 3 offering a menu of treatment options. Once AML was in the bloodstream, it was like that Beatles song: Here. There. And everywhere.

Frightening descriptions ("malignant," "fast-growing," "can get worse quickly") abounded. But the different sites were coy about what I really wanted to know: survival rates. One site promisingly offered that the first round of chemo resulted in remission in 50 percent of adults over age sixty. Another stated that only 5 to 15 percent of those older than sixty were likely to survive without relapse over the long term. But was relapse synonymous with death? Many links later, I finally found a flat-out survival rate for men in Joe's age group: one in eight. Getting out my calculator, I quickly divided one by eight. *Wait, that can't be right.* I cleared the screen and this time pressed the keys more deliberately. One divided by eight equals...*Twelve percent?*

Too much information. I logged off and stepped away from the computer.

Over dinner, Joe and I tried to act like our world wasn't

imploding, but Becky sensed something was wrong. "Is Daddy all right?" she asked more than once. Seeing an opportunity to lay a little groundwork, I told her that in the morning we would receive the results of some blood tests Daddy had taken. "Hopefully, it's just a virus," I said. "But if it's something else, we'll all deal with it." Becky was satisfied with that answer. Joe's nod signaled he was, too.

While Becky bathed, Joe and I pooled our research (though I kept that one-in-eight statistic to myself), then overrode our tell-no-one decision and phoned my sister-in-law Lou Anna, a nurse practitioner. As we'd hoped, she helped us prepare a thorough list of questions for our meeting with Dr. B. But Lou Anna's greater gift proved to be her reaction to Joe's diagnosis. In a tone both matter-of-fact and inflected with the same upbeat energy she brings to any exchange, she said, "Well, now we know what we're dealing with." In the moment, I found her emotion-free reply steadying; in time, I would come to regard it as the gold standard of responses. While acknowledging Joe's condition, it neither lent to our upset nor required a response. And it was positive, something that inched the situation forward.

Later that night, Joe sounded winded as he tossed beside me in bed. Just twenty-four hours earlier I'd noticed his breathing had a shallow choppiness that resembled his aging, anemic mother's, but I'd thought nothing of it. Now, his every breath stirred concern. Each time he made a bathroom run, I grew anxious. Finally, he settled down, and we rolled into each other's arms. "Feel sorry for yourself tonight," I whispered, "but tomorrow you have to come out fighting."

Hours after Joe dozed off, I gave up on sleep and tiptoed downstairs, thinking, *I need to tell someone.* The minute my younger brother,

Jonathan, came on the line, I burst into tears. When his groggy gasp gave way to, "Oh, Meus, oh, Meus" (the nickname the four Smolowe sibs call all but the youngest of us), I got off the phone quickly, feeling only worse for having woken him at 4:00 a.m. on a workday.

Still in need of release, I turned to my computer and pounded out three single-spaced journal pages. I made a list of people Joe and I knew who'd dealt with cancer and might be able to provide helpful information. I considered tracking down an old high school friend whose father had died when she was thirteen. I thought about getting a Paxil prescription to stave off depression. I worried about the logistics of getting Joe in and out of Manhattan for treatment. I wondered if Joe would need either a bone marrow transplant or its modern equivalent, a stem cell transplant; if I was a potential donor; if my being a donor might be too risky, given Becky. I noted my frustration with Dr. B's withholding of information. And I confronted my emotions head-on.

I keep thinking, This is not believable. Then I cry. Then I go to the extreme and can't imagine my life without him. I notice that while his first reaction is to wither, mine is to fight. We're both in shock. Hopefully, his first reactions are just that and no more. He said, "I guess I'm officially in retirement now. Time to tap the IRA." He's always fought the idea of dipping into that account . . . I was impressed with how Lou Anna didn't overreact . . .No expressions of how sorry she was, gasps of horror, etc. As she was talking, I was thinking about a phone call I had with [my college friend] Richard before Xmas where I learned his wife had died two years ago. As I heard myself repeatedly saying, "Oh, Richard, I'm so sorry," I felt I was being a burden. Now, I know I was. There is no good response, but that sure as hell isn't it. I just called Jonathan. It was a mistake. What the hell could he say? What the hell did I need to hear? Today, after Dr. B, we're going to go through that again and again as we let family know. I'd rather not. What would be useful? People delivering meals. Now that would be useful.

What I want right now is for my mind to keep moving, not get locked into this 24/7. Depression will do Joe, Becky, and me no good. I keep hearing a snippet of an old song, "It's a turn down day." Don't even know what that means. Gloomy words, cheerful tune . . . I finished [an old friend's] new book yesterday. Near the end, he has an email address. I thought, I'll write him. Now, do I write? That's the kind of thinking that's dangerous. Life needs to go on . . . This is very, very bad. Any fantasies I've ever had about dire circumstances have involved relief/respite at telling others. I already know better. Talking about this, just saying the word leukemia, is a trigger to cry. Not useful. Gotta be strong. For Becky. For Joe. Joe has long had a fear I'd be too quick to "pull the plug." Now, it's the reverse: I'm afraid he'll cave to his fear. Let his imagination run away with dark fantasy. I need Joe to be tough and determined.

The next morning while Joe did his sit-ups, I went for a speed walk. Usually when I exercise, I get lost in the music playing on my iPod. Now, I was deaf to the tracks as tears blurred my vision and the image of a huge, black abyss clouded my mind. When a stark thought crystallized—*If he goes, I'm going to have to reimagine my whole life*—I began to sob.

Before returning home, I got my emotions under control, determined not to exacerbate Joe's fears. We showered and dressed, saw Becky off to school, then drove into the city. While Joe sat in Dr. B's waiting area, I slipped into the corridor to phone my editor at *People*, where I was a senior writer and Joe was once executive editor. The mom-friendly, two-day-a-week schedule that I'd negotiated years earlier required me to be in the office on the magazine's busiest days. This was one of those days; deadlines don't wait. When I told my editor why I had to be absent on such short notice, she gasped and said, "Stay with Joe. Don't give work another thought."

Our meeting with Dr. B was informative, her manner straightforward as she outlined the treatment regimen. First up, a hospital stay of twenty-eight days for an "induction" round of "very intense and tough" chemotherapy. Designed to destroy Joe's rapidly multiplying leukemic cells, the chemo would obliterate his immune system as it sent the counts of his red blood cells, white blood cells, and platelets into freefall. If all went well, his counts would gradually climb back toward normal levels and a bone marrow biopsy would indicate that Joe was in remission. He'd then go home to continue rebuilding his blood counts and strength. Three "consolidation" rounds of in-hospital chemo would follow. After each, Joe would return home while his counts dropped; when the numbers began to bottom out, he'd be readmitted and quarantined until they reversed course. When we asked if a bone marrow transplant would follow, Dr. B said that Joe's age was prohibitive. If three rounds of consolidation therapy didn't leave him in remission, there would be a fourth; she doubted a transplant would be more effective.

"You don't have too much time," she said. "Treatment needs to begin right away."

Joe said he was inclined to check into Roosevelt, where Dr. B and his other doctors were affiliated, but first wanted to research other hospitals, particularly Memorial Sloan-Kettering. Dr. B responded that Sloan-Kettering had the advantage of deep experience; on the other hand, it treated so many leukemia patients that a person could feel like a number. If Joe checked into Roosevelt, she would personally oversee his treatment. Noting that the chemo protocol was "pretty standard," she added, with a wry smile, "People die at Memorial Sloan-Kettering, too."

As Joe and I laughed, he shot me a look that said, See why I like this woman? Yes, I understood. She had a sense of humor. She didn't make us feel rushed. Most important, she answered our questions, and in language we could understand. After Joe was shown out to have blood drawn, I welled up. Soundlessly, Dr. B placed a box of Kleenex in front of me, then stepped out of her office and closed the door. Yes, I liked this woman, too.

Before returning home, Joe and I dropped in on Dr. D, a cardiologist also affiliated with Roosevelt. Joe's primary physician for years and mine more recently, Dr. D was the physician who'd noticed the change in Joe's blood counts and ordered a second blood screen. A warm man whom we both trusted, Dr. D praised Dr. B as "a wonderful hematologist," and "a good communicator," a comment that affirmed our sense of her. Attuned to Joe's shock, he said, "Your self-control is incredible. I think you have the temperament to overcome this." Responsive to my concern, voiced out of Joe's earshot, that I was at risk of sinking into depression, he wrote me a prescription for Paxil.

The rest of the day was devoted to phone calls. First up: our families. While Joe informed his sister and, more difficult, his widowed mother, who at ninety-four was battling health issues of her own, I told my parents and three siblings. The reactions were just what you might imagine, Jonathan's included. (He'd been so sound asleep that he had no recollection of our predawn conversation.) Given so many muted gasps of horror, my sister Ann's overt shriek of, "Leukemia, Meus! Leukemia!" was peculiarly satisfying. Yes, goddamn it. Leukemia! There were expressions of bewilderment that a man so fit could be so sick. Offers of help. And question after concerned question. What did the diagnosis mean? What did the treatment involve? How was Joe reacting? How was I doing? What were we going to tell Becky?

Joe and I found it wrenching to cause so much distress; painful to absorb so much shock; draining to repeat the same information over and over; numbing to hear so many unsupported claims (an echo of my own the night before) that Joe would prevail; and exhausting to try to reassure everybody that we would get through this. By the end of the calls, we were so wrung out that neither of us ever wanted to say the word "leukemia" again.

But delay was not an option. Next, we tackled the calls we needed to place together. From our health insurance company we obtained a list of in-network hospitals and support services. We spoke with Becky's favorite middle-school teacher and secured his promise to alert us if he noticed any changes in her behavior. We also phoned our attorney, Grace. A few months earlier Joe and I had decided to alter our guardianship arrangements for Becky. While we'd secured the consent of the involved parties, we'd felt no rush to formalize the changes. Now, we told Grace, we had an urgent need to update our wills.

To my surprise, Joe also asked Grace to fax him a living will form. When we hung up, I reminded him that back when I'd signed my own, he'd been so uncomfortable with my liberal definition of "heroic measures" that I'd designated my older brother, Alan, as my health care proxy. Perhaps, I suggested, Joe might want a representative more in sync with his own wishes. He didn't. Quickly checking off his preferences, Joe designated me and signed. He then gave me the passwords to his cell phone, e-mail, and assorted bank accounts. Nowhere in any of this did we speak of death. But clearly the possibility was as much on Joe's mind as mine.

We then parted to place separate calls. Later, Joe would tell me that conversations with two of his friends who'd received cancer treatment at Memorial Sloan-Kettering had convinced him to stick with Dr. B. After I concurred, he notified Dr. B's office. That was soon followed by a call from Roosevelt providing a check-in time for the next morning.

Joe's other calls were to his editors at the two magazines where he was under contract for freelance work, and to a close friend on the West Coast. That friend quickly followed up with an e-mail supplying the name and phone number of his friend, Mary, who he said was a few months into treatment for AML and was willing to talk with Joe. Mary proved tremendously helpful. When I walked into Joe's office during their phone conversation, he seemed more like the Wease I knew: alert, attentive, his questions spiced with laughter. While talking to Mary, I think his dark fantasies were crowded aside by specific details about his pending treatment. In coming months, Joe and Mary would compare test results, medications, side effects, and doctor's pronouncements. Kindred leukemia patients, they could count on each other to understand the details and rigors of their highly specialized, very narrowed worlds.

My own phone calls began with my *People* editor, this time to let her know how quickly things were moving. "I'm not sure how soon I'll be able to come back," I said. Firmly, she told me to take all the time I needed. Then I phoned both Becky's former babysitter and my next-door neighbor. Each assured me she could step in at a moment's notice to look after Becky.

My final call was to my dearest friend, Lynn, whom I'd told about Joe's blood tests and was anticipating an update. My loving confidante since college days, Lynn has a keen intelligence and penetrating thoughtfulness that always makes her side of our ongoing dialogue interesting and insightful. But a crude indication of just how altered my reality had already become, I regretted placing the call the instant Lynn came on the line. As she launched into her usual probing questions, I began to squirm. I didn't want to repeat all the medical information. I didn't want to discuss hospital options. I didn't want to . . .Wait, what was that? Social Security? No, I hadn't thought of that. Was Joe eligible at sixty-four?

"I'll look into it and get back to you," she said.

I hung up, so grateful to have Lynn in my corner.

That left one person—in Joe's and my universe, the most important—who still needed to be told. During our chat with Dr. D, we'd asked how he thought we should break the news to Becky. "I would soft-pedal a little at this point," he said. Alternately, a friend had offered, "Becky *has* to be involved. Yours is a home where decisions have never been hidden. You can't start now." Joe and I were both more comfortable with the second approach. Smart and perceptive, Becky would sense if we were withholding something important from her. On the other hand, we didn't want to cause needless alarm. During our consultation with Dr. B, she'd cautioned, "Don't get ahead of yourselves. Just get on the train and go for the ride." Joe and I agreed that seemed apt advice for dealing with Becky. We'd present only what we knew for certain and steer clear of speculation.

Over dinner, we tried to emulate Lou Anna's matter-of-fact, upbeat tone as we laid out the "facts" for Becky. Daddy is sick. He has a cancer of the blood called leukemia. Tomorrow he will check into a Manhattan hospital to begin the first of four rounds of chemo. She will be able to visit Daddy the first weekend and may have to wear a mask over her nose and mouth because the chemo will quickly begin to destroy Daddy's immune system. After that, only Mommy will be allowed in his room because Daddy has to avoid contact with germs, which can cause infections. Between each chemo round, Daddy will come home. Any questions?

"Will Daddy lose his hair?" We nodded. "Why?"

"I don't know," Joe said. "Maybe you could research that online for us." Any other questions?

"Just let me know what's going on," Becky said.

As the conversation wound down, we told Becky we thought Daddy might return home for the first time in about four weeks. "Daddy should stay in the hospital until he's better so he doesn't pick up any infection at home," she said, her tone bearing a hint of, *Duh, guys, do I have to state the obvious?* Over her head, Joe and I exchanged a look of amazement.

In coming months, Becky would continue to be just what that response suggested: grounded, ungiven to emotional outbursts, mature beyond her years. She was—she is—truly amazing.

Later that evening, the phone rang. "So, what did you think of the party?"

It took me a second to identify the voice and understand the question. Right, Ken, one of my closest friends, one of Becky's two godfathers. The party? Right, New Year's Eve in Pennsylvania. "Hey, it was great," I said, struggling to sound convincing. It all felt so distant: the annual fete at Ken and Arthur's; our weekend life in rural Susquehanna County; my life, period. *Cut this short,* I told myself. Then, an idea popped into my head. "Hold on a sec," I said.

Dashing upstairs, I said to Joe, "Ken is on the phone. Can I tell him about your diagnosis and ask him to pass the news along to our Pennsylvania friends?"

Joe frowned. Throughout our marriage, we'd always dealt with our problems by turning toward each other and away from the world. But our many necessary phone calls that afternoon had already muddied the distinction between our public and private spheres. Our usual approach wasn't going to work. "There's no hiding this, Wease," I said. "And I can't keep telling people over and over. It's too draining."

Silently, Joe deliberated, his head wagging side to side. Then, he nodded. "Go ahead."

Having cared for people in the final stages of AIDS, Ken knew better than to press for details. Instead, he said, "What can we do?"

"Can you spread the word to the Pennsylvania crowd?"

"Done," he said.

That night in our darkened bedroom, Joe and I lay side by side, exhausted. In a single day, we'd done everything we could think of to pave the way for his protracted absence. Tomorrow, after I got Becky off to school and picked up a few toiletries for Joe's hospital stay, we would drive into Manhattan to enter the world of cancer treatment. Frightening as that prospect was, I felt relief that Joe would soon be in the full-time care of medical professionals. Now that his diagnosis had sunk in, Joe was no longer trying to ignore the symptoms he'd been experiencing for two months. With each passing hour, his body seemed to grow heavier with aches, chills, fever, and fatigue as his mind groped for meaning: Why me? Why this? Why now? What next? What if there is no next?

At some point, we turned into each other's arms. That Joe wanted to make love, let alone that he could, filled me with wonder. When the victory proved fleeting, I hugged him tight against my body and tilted my face away, not wanting him to feel the tears streaming down my cheeks, uncorked by the two chilling words that had entered my head: *death sex.*

2

ROAD MAP

Joe's hospital check-in was a mere formality. By then, he'd already entered a different universe—and so had I. It wasn't only my daily rhythms and assumptions about the future that had changed. So had the voices around me, which were now a relentless chorus of shock and concern. People didn't so much see *me* as they saw a dire situation onto which they projected their darkest fantasies. I understood the impulse. I'd done the same not only that day in the parking lot with Elizabeth, but also countless times after reading (or writing) articles about lives upended by calamity. How, I'd wonder, would I react to a natural disaster, a terrorist attack, a school shooting, a freak accident? Invariably, I arrived at the same conclusion: the question was unanswerable. Any event powerful enough to erase the familiar contours of my life would surely also erase the familiar responses I count on to see me through hard times.

Now that cataclysm had actually struck, I was experiencing an uncanny clarity that, indeed, I couldn't have predicted. I kept expecting to be fogged by dread and worry—yet my mind was clear and forward-thinking, a heightened lucidity that at the time I thought must be what soldiers experience when thrust suddenly into battle. No less unexpected was my reaction to the crush of pained looks, awkward hugs, and expressions of concern that greeted me at every turn. Rather than feeling comforted, I was agitated by the unfamiliar and unwanted attention, which rendered my shaken world even more unrecognizable.

In hindsight, I think *that's* why my internal messages were so loud and unambiguous in the days following Joe's diagnosis. Unlike the surrounding din, which reinforced my fears and magnified my new isolation, these messages spoke directly to what would help keep Joe, Becky, and me steady. Some, like my glimpse of myself as That Woman, were intuitive flashes that ordinarily might have gotten lost in the swirl of daily life. Others emerged during conversations or internal monologues that, in happier times, might not have commanded my undivided attention. But with so much at stake, I was closely attuned to what my instincts were telling me. I didn't debate, censor, or apply diplomatic pressure to these reactions. I just went with them.

I see now that what came through were sharp, precise reminders of who I am, how I navigate, how I cope best. These messages, key to rebounding from the shock of Joe's diagnosis—and, later, his death—were telling me that though circumstance had dramatically altered the outer landscape of my life, my inner landscape was largely unchanged.

On the first day, for instance, within seconds of hearing the *L* word I acknowledged my ignorance about the disease and sought information. When I realized we would gain no clarity until we knew Joe's type of leukemia, I prodded my stunned husband to call Dr. B back. This reaction was hardly surprising. As journalists, Joe and I were accustomed to asking questions, gathering information, and trying to shine a light on opaque situations under deadline conditions. The next morning when we arrived for the consult, I was wary of this doctor whom Joe liked. That, too, was characteristic.

Dr. B's initial reluctance to name Joe's illness, compounded by her failure to type it, had grated against my preference for straightforward answers. She dispelled my concern with her opening comment, a blend of straight talk and encouragement. "This is not a good diagnosis, but it's not impossible to treat," she said. "It's early." Later when I started to cry, her decision to slip into the hallway played to my keen sense of privacy.

As for my predawn call to my younger brother, that was a scene better suited to a made-for-TV weeper than my comfort zone. More typical of me was the guilt I felt for waking Jonathan so early on a workday. My subsequent impulse to vent my upset in a journal entry was truer to my normal coping mechanisms. More productive, too. Though I couldn't know it at the time, that entry drew a remarkably accurate road map of what I would need to handle the challenges ahead.

Three observations were particularly telling. The first came as I recalled how I'd reacted to my friend Richard's news of his wife's death. I saw a similar tide of sympathy rushing toward me and anticipated frustration, not consolation. No surprise there. When I'm distressed, my habit is to confide deeply in a few, seek input from people who have experienced a similar situation, and otherwise maintain my own counsel. The second significant notation was my comment, *What I want right now is for my mind to keep moving, not get locked into this 24/7.* I've suffered two clinical depressions in my life. Both times, the precipitating event, while deeply upsetting, was not as traumatizing as the resulting depression, which totally rearranged my mind, outlook, and days. Each of those depressions had been preceded by a deepening anxiety that gradually straightjacketed my thinking. Thus, I was alert to the threat that nonstop discussion about Joe's illness might mire my thoughts in a repetitive groove, like a record player needle stuck on an album track. The third telling point? *I need Joe to be tough and determined.* While I'd never known my completist husband to step back from any challenge he'd undertaken, I'd seen how he could stall and stall when torn by indecision. This health crisis provided no time for deliberation. I needed him on board, *now.*

That thought went hand in hand with the thought that chilled me later that morning, then hovered for the next two and half years: *If he goes, I'm going to have to reimagine my whole life.* I was well aware that I had an amazing daughter, wonderful friends and family, a stable job, a lovely home, and the life skills needed to function without Joe. But I also knew this: the center of my life was my relationship with Joe, my commitment to our marriage its organizing principle. Strip away the *we* that informed all parts of my life, and I could not imagine the remaining *I.*

At the same time that my inner voice was speaking more assertively than usual, as if commanding, "Remember who you are," I was also listening more receptively to other people's input. Perhaps I understood that the stakes were way too high to let my ego stand in the way of useful guidance. Or maybe during the days before Joe's survival instinct kicked in, my own recognized that I couldn't wage this battle alone. I just know that when a suggestion felt right, it, too, came through loud and clear.

Two conversations made a particular impression. The first was with my sister, Ann, who drove from Vermont to New Jersey the day after Joe checked into Roosevelt, determined to lighten my load. She didn't ask if she could come; she simply announced what time she would arrive. She'd probably calculated—correctly—that had she sought my permission, I would have balked. With a full-time fund-raising job at Dartmouth College, a husband, two teenage kids, and a dog, my younger sister already had a surfeit of demands on her time and attention. Over the next few days, even as she stayed on top of her work via computer, magical Aunt Pooz kept Becky too distracted to overthink the Daddy situation, filling her nonschool hours with outings and sous-chef duties that helped fill our freezer with meals far tastier than my own. All of this was quintessential Pooz. Swoop in. Take charge. Accomplish a Herculean number of tasks without breaking a sweat. Slip quietly back out.

But Ann's greatest gift was something she said to me. Though the day she arrived had been exhausting, by the time I left the hospital Joe was showing encouraging signs of shaking off his stunned upset. On deck first thing the next morning: surgery to insert a catheter so he could begin chemo in the afternoon. Around 10:00 p.m., as Ann and I lay on the living room couches talking, Joe phoned sounding very upset. An X-ray had turned up a pneumonia spot on his lung. The surgery was off. Now his doctors were debating whether to go with a less invasive access line or send him home until the spot cleared. Joe was vehement; he did not want to postpone treatment.

Returning to the living room, I burst into tears as I told Ann what was happening and voiced concern that this setback might undermine Joe's building resolve.

"Maybe you should get a second opinion," Ann responded.

"Why?" I said. "Joe is already in the hospital."

"Other hospitals might read the situation differently."

She was right. But I knew Joe wouldn't want to rethink hospital options. As Ann and I went back and forth, my sister pressing her point, me resisting, I was reminded that Ann and her husband had a different way of tackling decision-making than Joe and I, whether buying a couch or settling on a course of medical treatment. Where she and Jim proceeded deliberatively, exploring and analyzing every option (call it the academic approach), Joe and I were more inclined to amass and absorb information quickly, make a decision, then move on without looking back (the daily deadline approach). Ordinarily, this difference between my sister and me didn't signify. Now, however, I felt my agitation rising. I did not want to talk about second opinions; I wanted to talk about Joe's upset and what I could do to keep it from chipping at his shaky resolve. When Ann tried to explain her position one time too many for my brittle patience, I said in a tone more snappish than I intended, "That's your way, not mine." I explained that while she and Jim might find reassurance in exploring alternatives, Joe took comfort from being surrounded by doctors he knew and trusted. I would do nothing to disturb that arrangement.

There was an icy frost in the air as Ann and I hugged and said good night. In bed, I tossed, feeling terrible. Ann had been trying to help; I'd been inexcusably brusque. The next morning when we met up in the kitchen for coffee, I launched into an apology: I knew she had nothing but my best interests at heart; she had driven all the way from Vermont to—

"Don't be ridiculous," she cut in. "I can't know what you need unless you tell me. What you said last night was helpful. I'm glad you told me."

In the moment, I was struck by her diplomacy, her forgiveness, her determination to open a window on my perspective rather than defend her own, all skills she'd polished during her many years as a business consultant. In coming days, I would gain a fuller appreciation of her response. This wasn't merely an attempt to smooth things between us. Overnight, Ann had revamped her approach to supporting me. Now, instead of viewing my situation through the lens of her own needs, she was viewing it through mine. I don't know how she managed this polar flip, but from that morning forward, my sister proved perfectly calibrated to what I needed at any given time.

Ann's response to our tiny skirmish proved critically instructive. It reminded that people are not mind readers; if I wanted support that I found useful, I would have to be explicit (albeit more politely) about my needs. Had I not spoken up, Ann unwittingly might have continued to offer suggestions I found stressful. That, in turn, might have provoked me, through no fault of Ann's, to turn away from my sister. At a time when she wanted to support me and I wanted to be able to lean on her, we instead could have disappointed, even hurt, each other.

The other critical conversation during these first days was with Richard, the college classmate mentioned in my journal entry hours after Joe's diagnosis. Given the nature of our relationship, I would not have anticipated that he'd have the greatest impact on my thinking. But for a variety of reasons, some dating back to our college days, some stretching back just weeks, he proved to be the right person at the right time. My ears were open; his heart was open. I heard him deeply. Intensely. Gratefully.

Though I'd known Richard since 1974, decades before Joe's diagnosis, we'd never been more than casual friends. Initially, we weren't even that. When I was a sophomore at Princeton, I made the mistake of signing up for a history course that presupposed—incorrectly, in my case—a familiarity with the most basic timeline of European events. Each week the large lecture audience broke into smaller units to discuss the assigned readings with an instructor. Unfortunately, I landed in the precept conducted by the lecturer, a renowned professor who treated the reading selections as a mere jumping-off point for more far-ranging discussion. Week after week, it wasn't only the professor who made me feel like the most ignorant person on the planet; Richard did, too. As the two of them would theorize, debate, and nod in mutual appreciation at ideas that sailed over my head, I grasped only that while the professor was annoyingly pompous, Richard was unfailingly courteous. At some point during the semester I learned that Richard, though just a sophomore, was already a star in the history department. That actually made me feel less stupid. If I was going to be intimidated, I'd picked the right guy.

Through the remainder of our undergraduate years, I admired Richard from afar. When the announcement came senior year that he'd won a prominent scholarship, I felt a personal satisfaction disproportionate to our nodding acquaintance. Here was empirical evidence that I had exquisite taste in people to feel daunted by. Richard went on to earn a law degree from another Ivy institution, to clerk for a Supreme Court justice, then to become the youngest faculty member at Harvard Law School. In coming decades, he would write brilliant books that routinely received glowing praise in the *New York Times Book Review*.

Only when our paths crossed in our early twenties did I discover that this soft-spoken intellectual giant was also a really nice guy. Meeting up with one of my favorite professors at a Manhattan restaurant, I was startled to see Richard at the table. I felt, well, honored to be included in such august company. Over the course of similar evenings that followed, I learned to enjoy Richard's company and relax around him (though "zoned out" might be a more accurate description when he and my former professor veered into fiery discussion about case law). During my midthirties, when my writing portfolio at *Time* magazine shifted from foreign affairs to criminal justice, I sometimes phoned Richard for comment. He was always good for a provocative quote, and I never felt I was breaching any ethical boundaries about sourcing. Richard and I were acquaintances, but it would have been presumptuous to claim him as a friend.

After I left *Time* in 1996, my contact with Richard shrank to the annual holiday dance: I'd send him a seasonal card showing Becky one year older; Richard would send a gracious handwritten response. When we reconnected at our twenty-fifth college reunion in 2002, I met his wife, Eve, a delightful oncologist, who chatted animatedly with Joe while Richard and I caught up. More years passed, then in early December 2006, soon after Joe and I mailed our holiday cards, the phone rang. "I had to call," Richard said. "I'm looking at this picture of your daughter. She's beautiful."

Well. We chatted about Becky. We chatted about our respective writing projects. We must have been a good fifteen, twenty minutes into our conversation when I said, "So, Richard, tell me about you. How's life?"

Calmly, he responded, "There's no good way to tell you this, so I'm just going to say it. My wife died two years ago."

I gasped. "Oh, my God, Richard. I'm so sorry."

As Richard talked me through the chronology from his wife's diagnosis of melanoma in 2000 to her death in April 2005, I kept up a persistent murmur of "Oh, Richard" and "I'm so sorry." *Shut up!* my brain screamed. *This isn't helping. She's gone almost two years. He's over his shock.* But Richard's news was so unexpected, so untimely, so just plain awful that I couldn't stop. "I know," he acknowledged each of my murmurs.

When he turned the conversation back to my life and asked, "How's Joe?" I surprised myself by offering information I'd shared only with family members and two close friends. "Actually, Joe has some weird stuff with his blood counts. We don't know what's the matter."

I think I was trying to connect with Richard, to say that at some level I understood what he was going through. But that was bullshit. His wife was dead. My husband was fine. Sure, there had been a series of funky blood tests, but Joe's diagnosis was still a month away; I had yet to entertain the possibility there might be something seriously wrong with him. Instantly, I regretted having cracked this door open. It felt diminishing of Richard's loss and pain. At conversation's end, when Richard said, "I hope everything turns out all right for Joe," I regretted it even more. His comment made the possibility of bad news feel too real. I pushed the thought away.

Richard, however, remained on my mind. A few days later, I asked my brother Jonathan if he'd known Richard at Princeton. Jonathan, who'd graduated a year behind us, answered, "Only by reputation. But I know from what you've said over the years how deeply you respect him." Those infrequent mentions were usually triggered by one of two events: either Richard had just published a book or there was a vacancy on the Supreme Court, always an occasion for me to trot out my firm conviction that the seat should go to Richard. Now I told Jonathan about Richard's wife. He responded with a shocked intake of breath. We were all barely out of our forties; this was a time for reaping, not burying.

Then the holidays descended, crowding thoughts of Richard from my mind. Shortly before the clock chimed 2007, a Pennsylvania friend said, "Aren't you glad 2006 is over? What a shitty year!" I was surprised to hear myself answer, "No, it was a good year. Everyone was healthy."

In hindsight, I think my conversation with Richard had awakened me to the possibility that all was not as it should be.

The day Joe checked into Roosevelt, a red blinking phone light greeted me as I came through the kitchen door around 8:00 p.m. Ignoring the waiting messages, I went in search of Becky and put her on the phone with Joe, who described his hospital room and explained why his chemo would be delivered intravenously. Becky, who's always hated shots, said this sounded much better than getting stuck with needles all the time. Listening to her deal so practically with such disturbing matters was steadying. By the time I tucked her into bed, it was past 10:00, too late to feel guilty about not returning calls. Dialing into the message system, I steeled for the outpouring of concern.

"Jill?" a familiar voice said. "It's Richard. I heard from your brother." After offering all of his phone numbers, he said he was available to talk whenever I felt ready, day or night.

Richard hadn't crossed my mind since Joe's diagnosis. Now, I thought, *Yes, this is just the person I want to talk to. Immediately.* Despite the late hour, I dialed Richard's home number. I don't remember how our conversation started, but I do know that it bypassed any sugarcoated reassurances about Joe's prospects and cut straight to truth-telling. The notes in my reporter's notebook indicate that I first asked about the toll chemo took on Richard's wife. "This chemo will be no fun," he said. "It fatigued Eve enormously."

Next, we compared the treatment protocols for melanoma and leukemia. I shared the jarring one-in-eight survival statistic I'd stumbled on. Richard did not offer any of the responses I'd heard from doctors and friends. ("Statistics are dated and misleading." "Joe is not a statistic." "If anyone can beat the odds, it's Joe.") Instead, Richard told me that at the time of Eve's diagnosis, her doctor told him she had five years. "That's what happened," he said, "almost to the day."

With that, Richard acknowledged the elephant that everyone else was stepping around or refusing to see, the one that for the last seventy-two hours had followed me from bed to shower, home to store, car to hospital. It was a relief someone else could see this elephant.

Still, Richard said, the early detection of Joe's leukemia "is extremely useful." He was trying to toss me a lifeline. When I didn't grab it, Richard threw the conversation wide open. "We can talk about anything you want," he said. "Anything."

That required no thought. "What I want to ask you is, How can I best help Joe?"

Richard was silent a moment. "Let me answer that by telling you the three things I regret most." First, he said, he wished he'd read more about melanoma. Because Eve was an oncologist, he figured she was better positioned to deal with the medical aspects of her condition. In hindsight, he wished he'd gained a firmer mastery of the details.

Next, "The God's honest truth, I wish that I had assumed the worst and had a conversation assuming there would be no more such conversations." Eve, optimistic to the end, might not have welcomed such a dialogue, he said, so "maybe this is a selfish voice speaking. Still, I wish I'd said, 'We don't know what will happen, so I want you to know,' and then just poured my heart out."

"Oh, Richard," I said. "I'm sure Eve knew you loved her."

As the words came out, I could hear how thin and meaningless they sounded—just like the comforting phrases I'd found so irksome over the past few days. What is this human impulse to rush in with bland reassurances about difficult circumstances that cannot be wished away? Why are we so averse to allowing people their pain?

"I know," Richard said. "But I still wish I'd been explicit, more articulate, more voluble."

But there had been obstacles: Eve's optimism, Richard's fear, and the stealthy course of death's approach. "Early on in our relationship she had Crohn's disease," he said. "Over the years, I must have seen her operated on ten times." No matter what came her way, Eve, strong and determined, bounced back. Except for the periods of chemo treatment, she never appeared debilitated. "Up until Eve died, I hadn't thought much about death." The night she died, they'd attended an elegant fundraiser. "She was wearing a new dress and she was as radiant as she could be," he said. Late that night as they lay in bed, "There was this shake and this sound like nothing I'd ever heard before." Then she was gone, too late for Richard to speak his heart.

That led to Richard's third regret. In hindsight, he said, he wished he and his wife had leveled with their three children about Eve's illness. "She never said anything to the kids. I was too passive. We didn't talk about these things." Eve dealt with the one obvious manifestation, the loss of her hair, by modeling her new wigs for the kids and sternly telling them, "I don't want you to make any jokes about my hair." Their ten-year-old son and six-year-old twins were too young to know what questions to ask. "They sure ask about it now," Richard said. "On a number of occasions, they've said, 'Why didn't you or Mommy tell us?'" One of his kids remembers not clearing the dinner table after Eve asked him to put the dishes in the sink. "They say, 'We wish we had known. We would have treated her better.'"

Looking back, Richard said, he saw that he and Eve should have talked more with each other about her illness, the possibility of death, their kids' future. Instead, he said, "there was passivity and denial on my part. I just evaded things that should not have been evaded."

As our conversation wound down, I told Richard how much trouble I was having with other people's concern. "I know their intentions are kind and my inclination to pull away is ungracious," I said, "but I find all that emotion exhausting." Which reminds me, I said. "I want to apologize for how I responded on the phone when you told me about Eve's death. I knew it wasn't doing you any good, but I couldn't stop myself from saying, 'I'm so sorry' over and over. I felt terrible about it afterward."

"Please don't," Richard said. "I find the cards, the calls, people staying in touch tremendously comforting."

I thanked him for his candor. I thanked him for so generously sharing his experience and knowledge with me (and I thank him again now for letting me share it with you). "This was hard-earned," he replied. "It's a blessing to answer questions and be able to share it."

I took considerable guidance from that conversation. Richard's wish that he'd researched his wife's cancer more thoroughly rekindled my desire to get a handle on Joe's situation. After stumbling on that jolting one-in-eight statistic, I'd steered clear of the Internet. Since then, both Dr. B and Dr. D had cautioned Joe and me not to get ahead of ourselves. "If we dump a lot of information on you," Dr. D said, "it becomes overwhelming."

True. But after talking with Richard, I resumed my research. I entertained no illusions about gaining mastery over the material. I have no medical training; I lack a scientific bent. But Richard validated both my inclination to dive into the literature and to make notes every time a medical professional added new information. Already I'd discovered how discomfited doctors and nurses could be by the sight of a reporter's notebook. When asked, "What are you writing?" I responded that with so much information coming at Joe and me so fast, it was helpful to have notes to consult. Some seemed to get it; others looked wary. Richard's words convinced me this was their problem, not mine.

Richard's regret about not leveling with his kids was also reinforcing. While Joe and I were comfortable with our decision not to hide his diagnosis from Becky, parenting is not a science. Becky seemed concerned but not rattled by the news; then again, she often harbors inner turmoil behind a calm exterior. I couldn't dismiss the possibility that our decision to tell her about Daddy's leukemia was more selfish than wise. I was going to be at the hospital a lot in coming months. I needed her to understand why, for the first time in her young life, Daddy would have the greater claim on my time.

Richard's words eased that concern. Going forward, I continued to share important "facts" with Becky and steer clear of speculation or emotional commentary. I recall her being upset with me just once. At the time Joe's doctors were divided over the transplant option, and Becky picked up on my anxiety. "You're hiding something," she said. I'd planned on discussing transplants with her only if we decided to go forward with one. But when she demanded, "What's going on?" I told her, and her anger dissipated.

Other things that Richard shared would come back to me at crucial times in coming months and years. He told me, for instance, that two nights before her death, Eve suffered seizure-like shakes that propelled Richard to grab the phone. Before he could finish dialing 9-1-1, she came to and said in a scolding tone, "What are you doing?" He hung up, letting her aggravation override his instinct to get help. Twice that vignette would resurface from my memory bank, each time occasioned by a spike in Joe's temperature. Under medical instruction to get to an emergency room if his temperature hit 101 degrees, Joe was more inclined both times to wait and see if his fever notched beyond that point before heading into Manhattan. Remembering Eve, I overrode his hesitation, in one instance waking a friend at 4:00 a.m. to ask her to come stay with Becky while we made the pre-sunrise drive.

But the message that made the deepest impression was Richard's gut-wrenching wish that he had assumed the worst, "then just poured my heart out." That wasn't, as Richard had put it, a "selfish voice" speaking. That was the voice of grief. Of regret.

Of hard-earned wisdom. And in this moment when my heart and mind were in search of guidance, I heard it. That piece of advice would prove more valuable than any other during the long journey ahead.

3
SURRENDER

"Don't get ahead yourselves," Dr. B had advised. "Just get on the train and go for the ride." It sounded like good advice, but Joe and I didn't have a clue which train we'd boarded or what that ride would be.

We got a fast lesson when we got off the elevator at Roosevelt's oncology floor. As we approached the nurses' station, a bushy-bearded guy in a wheelchair at the far end of the hallway started screaming wildly. Shooting each other panicked looks, we quickly made our way to Joe's assigned room. On one side was a freshly made bed; on the other a freshman-dorm montage of rumpled sheets, soiled clothes and opened food packets, crumbs spewed across the mattress and floor. As our eyes telegraphed mutual *What the fuck?* dismay, a voice behind us boomed, "Hey, are you my new roomie?" There was the guy in the wheelchair, who met our stunned expressions with a loud cackle, then rolled away. Color draining from his face, Joe sank onto a metal chair.

"I'll be right back," I said.

Dr. B had told us that on the top floor there were expensive private rooms, uncovered by health insurance. "There's nothing you'll get up there that you won't get on the oncology floor," she'd said. "We're not the pampered types," I'd responded. Now, I rode the elevator to the top floor and stepped out into an oasis of calm. Carpeted hallways muted the sounds of rolling carts, beds, and

IV poles. Each room was clean and appointed in the manner of a midlevel hotel chain room: TV and DVD player; small fridge; private bathroom; comfortable reclining lounger for the patient, cushioned straight-back chair for visitors; large windows that provided a feeling of airiness. The cheapest room went for four hundred dollars a day.

"I'll take it," I said.

Joe was still sitting in the chair, staring at the floor, when I returned and told him what I'd done. "Are you sure, Wease?" he said. "Can we afford this?"

"I'd drain our savings accounts, our IRAs, even Becky's college fund if it will help you get better," I said. "What's any of it worth without you?" Then I rousted him out of the room.

Years later when my father had surgery at a hospital in North Carolina, I discovered that luxury accommodations in a large urban hospital are standard fare in a smaller regional facility. Minus the wallpaper and curtains, my dad's room had the same features, only his recliner offered more options. It's probably just as well Joe and I didn't know this at the time. The stark contrast between Roosevelt's disheveled double and the quiet, super-sanitized single provided an invaluable lesson in relativity for both of us. Yes, what we were facing sucked—but now we knew it could be a hell of a lot worse.

In coming hours as assorted doctors rotated through the room, asking the same questions over and over, Joe began to ease into his new patient role. The existential "Why me? Why this?" litany disappeared, never to return, and his charm began to rekindle. He showed interest in the procedures that lay ahead, the people who would be treating him, and the role he could play to help the effort along.

For both of us, the little drama had thrown into relief how much we valued our privacy, and how fortunate we were to be able to afford it in this difficult setting. For Joe, who at times had accused me of penny-pinching, I think my unilateral decision to spring for the private room drove home that we were in this together; there was nothing I wouldn't do to help him get well.

Over the next two days, flashes of Joe's humor resurfaced as he was prepped for chemo. When a nervous intern with a blonde ponytail splattered his blood all over a wall while inserting a needle, we laughed and hunted for images in the resulting stain. When flowers arrived from friends who hadn't gotten word that germ-bearing plants weren't allowed, a longstanding joke enabled us to laugh about cancer for the first time. A master of very-Jill gifts on birthdays, anniversaries, and holidays, Joe took pride in never having given me flowers. "Too trite," he'd insist whenever I asked, with mock distress, "What does it take for a girl to get flowers?" Now, when I quipped, "Apparently it takes leukemia," his face lit up.

Soon after his first chemo cocktail began to flow, Joe let loose with a loud fart. "Okay, Wease," he whispered. "This is the chemo." We cracked up. A half hour later he couldn't find his reading glasses, an absent-minded habit that even in the best of times made for frantic daily searches. How, I wondered, was it possible to lose a pair of glasses in a hospital room? "It's the chemo," he answered soberly. When he again burst into his familiar laugh, I felt my confidence in him revive. Over the next few hours as the bags of toxins drained without provoking nausea, I could see Joe's reviving, too.

Afterwards, looking relaxed for the first time since his diagnosis, Joe asked me, also for the first time since his diagnosis, "How are you doing, Wease?" For the last four days, I'd been so careful to show Joe steadiness and calm. Now, I spoke candidly. "I'd rather be where you are," I said, pointing to the bed. "I'd rather be facing the possibility of going."

Joe's head jerked, his expression startled. "Why?"

"Because if you go—" I shrugged. "Well, then you're gone. But me? I'll have to reimagine my whole life. And that terrifies me."

There. It was finally out in the open, the matter foremost in both our minds: death. Only now did it occur to Joe that I might be as shaken and in need of reassurance as he was. "Did I ever tell you about the train ride I took with my first wife?" he said. "We rode from St. Louis to Mexico City. It was long, but we got there. Think of this as a long, but doable ride."

Finally, I was looking at the husband I knew. The echo of Dr. B's train analogy suggested that through his fog of shock Joe had been absorbing information about what lay ahead. That he regarded the ride as "doable" suggested that his completist streak was resurging. Relief coursed through me. I hadn't realized how much I'd been missing Joe and longing to talk to him.

I recounted my conversation with Richard two days earlier, recapping his three regrets, among them his wish that he had "assumed the worst," then poured his heart out. While Richard had doubted that Eve would have welcomed such frank talk, Joe seemed relieved to be talking candidly, both of us crying as we shared our darkest thoughts. Given his age, we agreed, it was impossible to pretend death wasn't a possibility. We talked about the disruptions ahead and what they would mean for Joe, for me, and especially for our daughter. It eased my anxiety to discuss my concerns with the one person as attuned to Becky's subtle, non-verbal reactions as I.

Who else, for that matter, could I level with about Joe's and my altered universe? Friends and relatives were so relentlessly optimistic about his prospects. Each time I heard that Joe was fit and youthful, it deepened my sense of isolation. No one else was dealing with the terrified guy I'd been tending for the last four days. "Everyone is so 'He's going to pull through this' rah-rah," I said. "I don't find that at all helpful."

"I know," Joe said. "Every time someone says they're praying for me or, 'I know you're going to beat this,' it makes me feel more sick. What I hear is they think I'm going to die."

"I find all that sympathy draining," I said. "I feel like I have to reassure everyone. It takes too much energy."

Joe said he felt the same way. He wanted to keep the world at bay so he could focus solely on recovering. To cut down on risk of infection, he wanted no visitors except me and, on days when he didn't look too ghastly, Becky. To preserve whatever strength remained while chemicals ravaged his immune system, he also didn't want to deal with phone calls. "Don't give anyone the number to this room," he said.

Our conversation restored us to a couple I recognized. Open. Honest. Disinclined to hide from each other. We'd finally boarded the train and, though neither of us knew where we were headed, I felt reassured. Wease was back. We would be making this journey together.

"You focus on getting well," I told him. "I'll handle everything else."

We were so lucky, Joe and I. Thanks to the supportive friends and relatives who stepped in to help keep Becky's life as normal as possible, I was able over the next five months to spend hours with Joe pretty much every day of his lengthy hospitalizations. On Mondays and Fridays, the days I wrote for *People*, I'd zoom into Manhattan early in the morning to spend an hour with him before work; if I didn't get out of work too late, I'd return at night for another hour.

The other five days of the week, I was with him eight to ten hours a day.

During these months, the comment I heard most frequently was, "Joe is so lucky to have you," often delivered in a reverent tone that suggested I was a paragon of selflessness. Nothing could have been further from the truth. There was nowhere else I wanted to be. Away from Joe, my mind would fill with dark imaginings, particularly during the first chemo round when we were new to the ups and downs of his treatment. Only when Joe was right in front of me did my fears ease.

I was keenly aware that Joe's wasn't the only life on the line. So was mine, the one I'd built with Wease and desperately did not want to lose. That realization stripped the nuanced grays from my life, leaving me in a dichromatic universe of stark blacks and whites. The way I saw it, I had two clearly defined roles. As Joe's caregiver, my job was to run errands and monitor the parade of doctors, nurses, fellows, residents, interns, externs (yes, there's really such a position), food service personnel, and cleaning staffers who cycled through his room, making sure they washed their hands and responded to Joe's needs. As Joe's sole visitor, my job was to bring fresh energy into the room each morning and continue to buck him up throughout the day. Neither role was difficult, but both were exhausting.

Away from the hospital, I didn't want to expend energy on anything that didn't replenish my reserves. If I felt what somebody was offering by way of encouragement or distraction would refortify the strength I needed for Joe, I accepted it. If I felt someone's good intentions risked draining me further, I declined the invitation or found an excuse to slip away.

There was only one fellow traveler in my new universe. Only one other person who saw things the same way I did. Only one person who didn't require explanations to understand my priorities, feelings, and needs. Being with Joe those eight, ten hours each day was exhausting, yes, but it wasn't a hardship. It was a relief.

Up to this point in our relationship, Joe and I, like any married couple, had withstood our share of battles. Over the years, the triggers had varied: Would we relocate for a job? Have children? Move to the suburbs? Who would cook dinner? Run the carpool? Walk the dog? Large or small, our differences almost always had the same essential issue at heart: Whose time needs took precedence?

Now, there was no his time, no my time. It was all our time, and for both of us every minute of every day was trained on the same goal: getting Joe through this. While there was plenty of fear, worry, and pain in his hospital room, there was no tension. We had no clashing agendas or rival priorities. No need to make allowances, concessions, or compromises. No expectations of the other, and therefore no disappointments. *Being together is easy,* I wrote in my journal. *I sense Joe's need to have me there, and that's enough love and reward in itself.*

For the first time in our twenty-five years together, we were in perfect sync. Disinclined to strain against the demands of his treatment, we slipped into a mutual state of surrender, each day dealing with exactly what was in front of us, and nothing more. We regarded Joe's treatment as a process that could not be rushed, its bumpy trajectory a roller-coaster ride that could not be avoided. When Joe's blood counts would plummet and his strength would flatline, we understood that it was part of the chemo cycle and waited patiently for his counts to rebound. Neither of us asked, Why this? Why us? Instead, we focused on getting through whatever it was.

While we didn't fill our days dwelling on our fears, neither of us hid from them or hid them from each other when unexpected developments landed us in scary new terrain. *Joe and I are both on the same page about feeling and acknowledging our fears*, I wrote.

At no point did Joe or I refer to him as a cancer "victim." We also steered clear of language I heard routinely outside his room, things like he was "waging the fight of his life" and would "beat this thing." In the initial shock of Joe's diagnosis, I, too, had cast him as a warrior. But after Joe signaled he'd do all he could to help his body mend, such phrases fell out of our discussion. To our ears, they suggested Joe was responsible for the outcome. We did not believe he had brought cancer on himself; we did not believe he could wish it away by summoning mental images of him slaying misshaped cells. *Neither of us is inclined toward the Think-Happy-Thoughts school of coping. A recent study showed that attitude did not change outcomes.* In our view, leukemia wasn't a self-inflicted punishment; it was a disease. Anything he or I could do to help his recovery along, we would do. But we understood the outcome was out of our hands.

The side effects, too. Suffice it to say, the hospital environment and Joe's medications kicked up a long list of unscheduled challenges, among them pneumonia, phlebitis, and blood clots. The damage to his gastrointestinal tract was so severe that it required surgery. Little of this threw us off balance, and when it did, we strove to regain perspective. After a sudden spike in fever proved to be a life-threatening case of E. coli bacteria infection, I wrote, *I feel like a melodrama queen when I let myself think he could die. I yank my thoughts back, telling myself, He ain't dead yet*. More typically, we reminded each other, "It is what it is." And then we dealt with whatever it was.

This was hardly typical behavior for two Type A personalities, my own marked by an inclination to be direct, impatient, decisive, and averse to ambiguity, Joe's by a tendency to be preoccupied,

focused, determined, and workaholic. Between us, we had an over-
abundance of Type A persistence, drive, and independence, and,
at sixty-four and fifty-one, respectively, enough experience with
dashed goals to appreciate the importance of having a backup plan.
Now, there was no Plan B. Beyond my showing up each morning
so we could proceed through the day together, there was no plan
at all. Becky apart, the only thing that mattered to either of us
was this dose of medicine. This procedure. This blood count. This
biopsy. This transfusion. For the first time in our lives, Joe and I
were mindful of each moment. Minute to minute, hour to hour,
day to day.

In the way of all hospital life, ours was a largely predictable existence that chugged along at one of three speeds: boring, more
boring, most boring. Quickly we came to appreciate that boring
was good. If a day wasn't boring, it usually meant Joe's health had
kicked up an unanticipated complication.

What we referred to as our New Normal seldom varied.
Each morning around 10:00 (on *People* days 7:00) I'd head into
Manhattan. An hour or so later, I'd pause outside Joe's hospital
room to shake off any lingering irritation from the often-frustrating
commute, then step through his door smiling. "Hi, Wease," I'd say,
my tone upbeat.

At the sound of my voice, Joe, already out of bed and seated in
the lounge chair either eating breakfast or reading the *New York
Times,* would look up, a smile lighting his eyes that left no doubt
that he'd been waiting for me. "Hi, Wease," he'd reply, and offer his
lips for a kiss.

No matter what the temperature outside, I then changed into
the shorts and t-shirt I kept in his room where, no matter which

way I turned the radiator dial, it was too cold for Joe's immune-compromised body and too hot for my menopause-compromised one. After handing Joe a folder filled with printouts of the day's e-mails from family and friends, I settled in the guest chair. That pretty much exhausted my plans for the day. Unless there was a scheduled procedure or X-ray, that pretty much exhausted Joe's, too.

Because Joe's doctors preferred him to sit upright, he remained in that chair all day, no matter how shitty he felt. If he was having a bad day, he dozed on and off, each time awaking with a "Hi, Wease." If he was having a good day, he'd do a Sudoku puzzle while I worked a crossword. I'd share news of Becky and other people in our distant outside world. We'd discuss the latest headlines and fume about whatever the Bush administration was up to. Though I always came armed with books and magazines, they rarely got touched; even on Joe's best days, I had neither the interest nor the concentration to wade in.

Quickly, we fell into a habit of saying, "I love you," each time I left the room, no matter how brief the errand. Unspoken between us was the obvious: if, God forbid, this was the last time we saw each other, we wanted an expression of love to be our parting exchange.

Mid-morning, a waiter would arrive with a lunch menu, which Joe would study at great length. I'd go downstairs to a deli to pick up my own lunch, usually a chicken salad or yogurt topped with granola. When Joe's meal arrived he would either eat with relish or push the tray away. That would be my cue to step in and coax him to try some Jell-O. Orange, today. Yum.

On Joe's better days, we'd follow lunch with a walk, his doctors having indicated that exercise helped. Slowly, we'd make our way down the corridors, pausing at each bank of windows to see if the water towers perched atop the high-rises offered anything new. (They never did.) Along the way, we either cursed the way the wheels on the damn IV pole impeded his progress or marveled that a new pole was doing what it was supposed to do. During these strolls, I'd case empty rooms for useful objects (like a better IV pole), which I would later sneak back into Joe's room to an admiring, "Wow, Wease!"

Since there was never anything to do but sit and wait for we-didn't-know-what, we were never in a rush to be anywhere and we were never engaged in an activity that couldn't be readily set aside. Any distraction was welcome: the nurses who periodically checked Joe's vitals, the doctors who repeatedly reviewed Joe's medical history. Whatever their question, Joe was always polite, thorough, and seemingly fascinated by his own responses. Most of the time I listened to make sure he left nothing out. But sometimes I didn't. Hey, can't you see I'm terribly busy working on this crossword puzzle?

Of course, we talked endlessly about every aspect of Joe's health and treatment: his blood counts, his bruises, his X-rays, his biopsies, his medications, his constipation, his balding pate. Joe's absorption with his ravaged body could be mind-numbing. Yet his tone never bore a trace of self-pity. Joe was a completist, not a complainer.

Given any excuse to laugh, we seized on it. Repeatedly, we marveled at the absurdly attractive cast of young interns and residents that rotated through the room. Was it possible good looks were a prerequisite to work in this unit? One resident, a ringer for McDreamy on *Grey's Anatomy* (only this guy was better because he had a cute French accent) responded to our consternation about a yellow spot on Joe's thigh ("Could it be gangrene?") by wetting a paper towel and rubbing it off. This left us in stitches. So did Joe's half-asleep attempt to pee into a plastic bottle, spraying urine all over the floor. His little mishap earned us a transfer to a huge room complete with a couch and work table. Hey, score!

Whenever Dr. B or her fellow entered the room, we snapped to attention, Joe sitting taller in his chair, me grabbing my reporter's notebook. Usually they had little more to report than Joe's latest blood counts. The day the ponytailed intern splattered Joe's blood on a wall, Dr. B told us sternly, "If any resident or intern wants to do anything more than take blood or your temperature, page me." Dutifully, I wrote her instruction in my notebook. On the few occasions we took her up on her offer, Dr. B, as promised, appeared within minutes. As a result, Joe and I were slavishly devoted to Dr. B and joked that our fondness for her was a warped version of Stockholm syndrome.

The highlight of each day came around 3:00 p.m. when the food staff set out coffee and platters of snacks in the visitors' lounge. I'd wander down and come back to the room armed with cookies. On the days Joe nibbled at one, I was thrilled that my husband, who used to down whole boxes of Fig Newtons in a single sitting, showed signs of an appetite. After choosing from among the DVDs sent by friends, Joe would climb onto the bed, I'd kill the lights and settle on the floor against a bank of pillows, and for the next two hours we'd try to lose ourselves in the movie du jour. The sillier the film, the worse the day Joe was having.

Once or twice a week as twilight darkened the sky outside Joe's windows, Dr. B would drop by, shrug off her overcoat and settle into the guest chair. For twenty or so minutes, the three of us would chat about films, books, theatre, the media, Dr. B's country place, her weekend plans with her husband. Joe and I flattered ourselves that we were Dr. B's "evening cocktail," but we suspected her visits were really designed to prop up our spirits. When she would put her coat back on, we felt like we were watching our old life walk out the door.

During the closing hour of our shared day, Joe would call home to chat with Becky. Afterwards, on weekdays, Joe would reach for

the remote at 7:00 and we'd watch *Jeopardy*. Then I'd change back
into my street clothes and kiss Joe's brow.

"I love you, Wease," I'd say.

"I love you, too, Wease," he'd reply.

Though that repetitive refrain never devolved into a routine
exchange or lost its power to touch, our expressions of love weren't
the main element that made the monotonously long days tolerable
for me. Joe and I had always been an affectionate couple, disinclined to taking our lively, loving dynamic for granted. Neither of
us had needed the wake-up call of leukemia to realize what we had
and what we stood to lose. A quarter century into our relationship,
we still enjoyed debating politics and ethics, discussing movies
and books, dissecting bosses' and friends' motives and behavior.
Twelve years into parenting, we still thrilled to the amusements
and challenges of raising our daughter. Together, we were looking
forward to our retirement years, when we would be untethered to
an office and have more time for travel, creative writing projects,
and each other. Each year on our anniversary, we'd recall the rogu-
ish friends who at our wedding reception had wagered how long
we'd last, then we would clink wine glasses and offer our annual
amused toast: "Fuck 'em if they can't take a joke."

Rather, what most sustained me during these months was
the keen feeling of appreciation that flowed between us. Joe's
short-lived defeatism after his diagnosis left me with a constant
appreciation for his tenacity, optimism, and determination. I
beamed when Dr. B told him, after round one of chemo, "You
came through this like a champ." I welled with pride each time
one of his doctors called him a "model patient" or a "poster boy"
for leukemia patients.

Joe, in turn, never lost sight of all I was juggling as I honored my promise to "handle everything else." It wasn't only that I dealt with my job, Becky, Joe's phone calls and e-mails, and the mountain of hospital bills that dwarfed the usual stack of household bills. Before Joe checked into Roosevelt for the first time, he'd experienced the weight of people's concern. He appreciated that I shielded him from the sympathy and endless questions about his progress.

The only thing we took for granted was that both of us would want me at the hospital as many hours as I could manage. Joe's need for me to be there, my need to be with him, were such givens that it didn't occur to either of us it could be any other way. Then, midway through Joe's chemo, we heard about a friend on the West Coast who was about to undergo shoulder surgery. Accustomed to dealing with a husband who was a bit of a hypochondriac, she was concerned that her spouse's need for attention might hamper her own recovery, and had asked a friend to be on hand throughout the hospitalization, primarily to keep her husband at bay. That story opened our eyes to how different our experience could have been—and how fortunate we were to share a desire for each other's company.

One morning, during Joe's third round of chemo, I enter his room to find him in so much pain that he is, uncharacteristically, still in bed. It hurts to watch him wriggling and wincing on the mattress. He squirms left, then right; he raises his hips; he turns on his side. No matter which way he repositions his body he can't find relief. The chemo drugs always produce sores along Joe's gastrointestinal tract; now the damage has extended to his behind. "I feel like a rectal patient who happens to have leukemia," he tells me, his attempt at humor unconvincing.

It's a *People* day, but I can't bear to leave him this way. My editors have been so wonderfully accommodating. I am certain they will let me use one of my remaining vacation days. "Maybe I should stay," I say.

"No," Joe says. "Go to work."

I don't know what steels his tone. Maybe he's thinking how pissed he would have been during his editing years at *People* if a writer had failed to show up on a closing day. Maybe he's thinking, *Let's not risk messing up your good gig; we need your health insurance to cover these expensive treatments.* Or maybe he's thinking he'd rather tough this out alone than have his wife bedside, focused on his wretched butt.

I hesitate. Time is running out. Actually, time has already run out. Minutes ago, I should have traversed the four long blocks from Tenth Avenue to Sixth Avenue, and the nine short blocks from Fifty-Ninth Street to Fiftieth Street. "I'll stay in touch," I say, and kiss Wease good-bye. In the corridor, I beg one of the nurses, "Please. Keep an eye on him. He's in so much pain."

I hurry down Ninth Avenue, my usual long stride quickened by the writing assignment and deadline that await me. I've put four, maybe five, blocks behind when I pass a pharmacy with a display of medical supplies in the window. Walkers. Canes. Suddenly, I remember an oval pillow that I used years earlier following gynecological surgery—a soft, rubbery doughnut sort of thing that left my aching private parts free of pressure or friction. I hesitate a few seconds, aware that I'm running late on a day when it's inexcusable not to show up on time. Then I think of all the hours Joe will lie on that bed in so much pain. If this damn pillow can make a difference . . .

I dash in and describe what I'm looking for to the guy behind the counter. He lifts a long metal pincer and plucks a box from the top shelf. Sold. Back out on the street, I start to run. I enter Joe's room panting and thrust the box at him. "Here. See if this helps. Gotta go."

"Wease," he says, packing a lot into that one word. He understands closing days.

Late in the afternoon, my office phone rings and a male voice instructs me to come to the package desk. Weird. Usually packages are delivered to my office. When I find my way to the subterranean station, a woman points to a white box and says, "Those are for you." I peer inside and see flowers unlike any I'm familiar with. The gold and magenta tones are vivid, the fragrance unusual and lovely. *Huh?* I think. Then, *Joe?* Then, *Not possible.* The man has never given me flowers. True, his facial expression had telegraphed that he regarded my unexpected pillow delivery as some sort of above-and-beyond feat. But the man is in agony, for God's sake. Brief check-ins throughout the day have indicated no improvement in his pain level. It is inconceivable that on this of all days Joe could have stepped out of himself to think of me, let alone found the strength to pull his phone from a side table drawer, the energy to track down a florist, the concentration to choose an arrangement and produce a credit card number.

I detach the small envelope stapled to the cellophane wrapping and withdraw the note card. Though the handwriting is not Joe's, the message definitely is: "You are one wonderful Weasel. I love you."

Please don't misunderstand me. There is no bright side to leukemia. None. For the patient, the treatment is brutal, the side effects painful, a happy outcome far from guaranteed. For the caregiver, the demands are relentless, the juggling exhausting, the attendant fears constant. Friends and relatives were not wrong to gasp with horror and imagine my life hideously disarranged. But was Joe "lucky" to have me? In all my life, I have never felt my priorities so clear, my concerns so unambiguous and well-founded, my hours so well spent. I have never loved so generously. I have never felt so cherished.

Six years later, that yellowed note card remains tacked to my office bulletin board at eye level. I leave it there to remind me what it felt like to be so very, very loved. I leave it there to remind me what it meant to be fully present. Together in the hospital, Joe and I not only lived in the moment; we lived in the *same* moment, temperature reading to temperature reading, blood count to blood count, bone marrow biopsy to bone marrow biopsy. Only this. Only now. Only us.

In its way, it was very Zen.

4

RORSCHACH BLOT

THE REST OF MY LIFE? NOT SO ZEN.

The eight to ten hours I spent with Joe each day left limited time to deal with the other imperatives in my life. *People* obligations apart, there were four: Spend time with Becky. Keep our household running. Inform loved ones about Joe's progress. Replenish my depleted reserves so I could reenter Joe's room the next morning armed with energy and fresh conversation that would brighten his confinement. I knew that last one would be the most challenging given the worry and fear that climbed into bed with me each night. If such thoughts didn't ease during my other hours away from Joe, I risked sinking into depression. Quickly, I devised a strategy. When I exited Joe's room each evening, I had to leave behind my New Normal of blood counts, lab results, and side effects, and try to reconnect with my Old Normal, where talk of a soaring stock market, the newly unveiled iPhone, and Hillary Clinton's presidential prospects might supply the diversion I needed to recharge.

There was only one hitch: my Old Normal wasn't cooperating. As soon as the Joe-has-leukemia grapevine kicked in, so did a cultural script that was far more tenacious than I could have imagined. Though I never doubted people's good intentions, their responses were so uniform—and so uniformly draining—that initially I was too busy fending off what *wasn't* helpful to think about what might actually be of use.

[Phone message] Oh, my God, I just heard about Joe! I can't believe it. Listen, I'm here. Any time. If you need to talk to someone at three in the morning, I'm your person. I'm home now, but I'll be out from five to seven. So, call me now or after seven, okay?

My flash of intuition in the parking lot two days after Joe's diagnosis hadn't been wrong. Now, every encounter involved eyes scrunched with concern, murmurs of commiseration laden with pity, a gaze trained on my face, as if in search of some hidden truth. Less expected, my new standing as That Woman erased all the other roles I ordinarily play, among them friend, writer, colleague, neighbor, carpooling mom. Instead, people saw only the wife of a very sick man. And that allowed for only one conversation: How's Joe? How's Becky? How are *you*?

While I had no trouble surrendering to the constricted boundaries of my New Normal—this way lay recovery; what was there to resist?—I could not make peace with the shrunken contours of my old one. I didn't feel soothed by the constant reminders that my husband was deathly ill. I didn't feel fortified by the repetitive conversations that neither distracted from worry nor exercised other parts of my personality and brain. Within days of settling into the rhythms of Joe's treatment, I began to hunger for the variety of everyday chitchat, casual banter, lively debate, and intimate dialogue that normally give momentum to my life. But at a moment when I needed such interaction more than ever, I had to work harder than ever to find it.

You are welcome to call us for ANYTHING that we can do if you need it. And I mean it.

—a New Jersey friend

If you need ANYTHING...call anytime.

—a Pennsylvania friend

Everybody asks, 'Is there anything we can do?' But please know we do not ask idly. If you can think of any way at all that we could make this less stressful for you, Joe, and Becky, I will count on you to tell us.

—a California friend

Those were the first three e-mails to land after Joe's diagnosis. Soon, that trickle became a deluge. Though the outpouring of kindness touched me deeply, I found the unbounded offers of "anything" bewildering, even agitating. Still reeling, I could think of only one thing I needed: for Joe to get well. Who could give me that? I feared the barrage of solicitude might tip me further off balance. The phone calls to my parents and siblings had shown me that expressions of shock delivered a high-voltage zap to my solar plexus. They'd also shown me that people's concern triggered a need in me to allay that worry. But the effort to reassure others added to the weight already pressing on me.

As for the repetitive questions about Joe's diagnosis—well, let me put it this way. When I return from a vacation, the first person to inquire gets a detailed account: Fine meals! Whimsical misadventures! Charming native customs! The next gets an abbreviated recap: Three days in Prague, two in Budapest, one anecdote. By the third telling, I've got it down to, "Eastern Europe was fascinating. So, what have *you* been up to?" Now, as the same questions came at me day after day, I found the interest not only exhausting, but also delicate to navigate. If the person loved Joe, I didn't want to seem unmindful of his or her distress; if it was a more casual acquaintance, I didn't want to seem ungrateful for the concern. I understood that people's questions were a way of expressing affection for

Joe and for me. Certainly, no one intended to make me feel trapped in a nightmarish version of *Groundhog Day*. But that's how I felt in no time at all.

"How are *you* doing, Wease?" Joe asked at the end of the first hospital week.

"No one talks to me about George Bush anymore," I said.

Neither of us laughed.

Because I was the only person permitted to visit Joe (except on rare occasion), I was the gatekeeper for not only the messages going into his room, but also the messages coming back out. The first night I returned home from the hospital and no longer had Joe in my sights, I discovered the not-knowing was worse than the knowing; it left too much to the imagination. As a result, I felt a keen responsibility to keep family and close friends informed. But by the time I rolled into our driveway, fed and talked with Becky, then saw her off to bed, I was too exhausted to spend what remained of my evening recounting the day's events in phone call after phone call.

So the morning after Joe checked into Roosevelt, I slugged an e-mail Weasel Update and began, *Yesterday was a good day. Joe is now settled in a private room that is so nice that when he called Becky last night, he said, 'My hotel room is . . . um, I mean hospital room.'* I briefly described the medical procedures scheduled for the following day and reassured, *Dr. B dropped in three times last night, which made it feel personal.* Though the e-mail addresses listed at the top included Joe's sister, my parents and siblings, and three close friends, I felt I was speaking to an audience of one: Joe's frail mother, Short, who I knew was sitting in her Pasadena apartment worrying about her only son.

That e-mail chain would quickly grow, reaching across town to local friends, across the country to Joe's old high school and college pals, across the globe to far-flung journalism colleagues. Yet Short remained my audience when I sat down most mornings to write. I never forgot that while I could eyeball Joe and talk with his doctors, she could not. To avoid needless alarm, I kept the Updates brief, held medical details to a minimum, and reached for humor or optimism whenever possible. If the news was dreary, I waited a day or two until there was something more upbeat to offer, then reported that after a bad patch, Joe was on the mend. While I never lied, I often didn't share disturbing developments or graphic details (this being Joe's wish as well as mine). And as with Becky, so with the Update audience: no speculation about outcomes; no projections about what might lie ahead; just the facts, sprinkled with anecdotes about the absurdities of hospital life.

When I printed and delivered the first batch of responses to Joe, it was wonderful to see my modest husband so surprised and moved by the caring messages. *I think it lifts his spirit to know that so many people are pulling for/thinking of/caring about him*, I wrote in the next Update. *I know it certainly lifts mine.* Now when people asked, "What can I send?" I had a ready reply: "Write him an e-mail."

I continued to ply that refrain throughout Joe's many hospitalizations (some anticipated, some not). I also stuck to my system of hand-delivered printouts even after a friend clued me into the existence of patient websites where people could post messages. Internet reception in the hospital was spotty. And I feared a large audience might alter the intimate nature of people's messages. Instead, first thing each morning I handed Joe a fresh stack of e-mails, then while I pretended to read the newspaper, watched his expression as he absorbed the messages of encouragement and love. In a day that promised mostly boredom, those ten, fifteen minutes were often his happiest.

The Updates served a valuable purpose for me, as well. During the six months Joe was constantly hospitalized, I often didn't sleep well or awoke feeling anxious. For me, it was therapeutic to go from my bed to my computer and focus on composing a concise, upbeat message. (More therapeutic, actually, than the Paxil, which I soon discontinued, convinced that no self-obliterating haze was hovering.) The writing exercise not only kept my sense of humor from atrophying, but also compelled me to hold setbacks in perspective. The e-mails waiting in my inbox reminded me how fortunate Joe and I were to have so many caring people in our lives and provided the shot of adrenaline I needed to walk into Joe's room smiling. E-mail also provided the distance I needed from anxious facial expressions and ill-timed interruptions. Not yet worn down by the tedium and upsets of a long hospital day, I was happy to answer people's questions.

Otherwise, I wriggled away from the sympathy and concern, the scrutiny and curiosity, even the genuine offers of help. How's Joe? "Good, thanks. I'll tell him you were asking." It always felt rude, but I couldn't engage all that interest. I just couldn't. Early on, I thrilled when I had a shopping encounter with a Montclair acquaintance who plainly hadn't heard about Joe's diagnosis. "Hey!" she called across the checkout lines, with a wave. "How are you and Joe?"

"Fine!" I said brightly, waving back. It felt so normal. Just two busy moms running errands.

But that, of course, was a scene from the Old Normal script. The new one called for different lines, different stage directions.

> *Jill! [A Montclair mom I haven't seen in years hurries toward me] We just heard about Joe. It's terrible! My heart goes out to you.*

Thank you. [Gesture at school door] I'm heading
inside to pick up Becky.

That's okay. Just tell me real quick. How's Becky
holding up?

She's a trouper.

[Concerned frown] And how are you doing?

Good, thanks. [Edge toward door] Gotta run.
Becky's waiting for me.

Yes, but—

I understood the assumptions underlying such oddly timed exchanges. That long-ago day when I spotted Elizabeth in the parking lot, I saw only pain and exhaustion etched in her face and couldn't imagine she might be thinking of anything but issues connected to her husband's illness. Weren't people just as unlikely to read aggravation about a clogged sink drain or the state of US policy in Iraq into the lines creasing my face? Many people, no doubt, felt compelled to ask about Joe because they thought I'd think it insensitive if they *didn't* inquire. (They weren't entirely wrong. In time, I grew uneasy with the few neighbors who never said a word.)

But the bombardment of hit-and-run conversations exacted a steep toll. As it was, my thoughts were never more than a few minutes from Joe, and thoughts of Joe were pretty much synonymous with worry. So when people would stop me, anywhere, anytime, to ask, "How's Joe? How are *you*?" it had the effect of ending my brief respite. Seconds later when they walked away, I'd be left tunneling my way out of the one place I didn't want to be: worrying about Joe. A warning that a traffic cop was in the area dispensing parking tickets or a comment about the overcast sky would have been more welcome. Such moments moved the dial off Joe, reminding me there was a larger world he and I would rejoin when—

Jill! Hi! I've been meaning to call you. How's Joe?
He's doing well, thanks. [Nudge cart down grocery aisle]
No, really. How is he.
Good. Hey, do you know where they moved the salad dressing?
God, I can't imagine.

That's true, you can't, not unless you've been through something similar or you're an A-list celebrity, accustomed to stares and relentless encroachments on your private life. Many people don't find the persistent questions as intrusive and enervating as I did. But I discovered shortly before Joe's stem cell transplant that my reaction was not unique.

While undergoing chemo, Joe had been put in touch with John, a West Coast leukemia patient in his midthirties. At parallel points in their treatment, Joe and John compared notes from time to time. One evening, I spoke by phone with John's wife, Heidi. Our universes, I learned, were parallel, too. Like me, Heidi was spending her days with her husband, keeping an eagle eye on his mood, medications, and minute-to-minute needs. At night, she faced a similar mountain of hospital bills, e-mails, and phone messages. To communicate with John's legion of supporters, she'd established a blog that informed people about John's progress and a Web page where friends could sign up to provide dinners.

But Heidi was dealing with a situation far more complicated than mine. Where Joe was approaching his transplant in good physical shape and had an exact donor match in his sister, John was not doing well and had a less precise match. Additionally, I had one child, a tweenager, who early on had told me, "I *want* you to be with Daddy." Heidi had three young children, one of them autistic, all of them clamoring for her attention. When I asked how she was reacting to people's concern, our conversation turned from a dialogue into a one-sided diatribe. Heidi hated—absolutely hated—the constant questions. During a recent grocery run, she said, "We were in the milk department and this woman comes up and asks, 'How's John?' I'm standing there with my three kids! How could she be so inconsiderate?" Heidi was furious that someone would raise such a difficult and complex issue in front of her children. "Everything people need to know is right there on my blog," she said. "Why don't people get it?" The encounter had spurred her to post a blunt message: Do *not* ask about John when my kids are around. Heidi had no qualms about cutting off unwanted questions. "When I'm out doing things that feel normal," she said, "it's like someone jerking you back when they ask."

For me, the conversation was a stress reliever. *It makes me feel less guilty that I'm not appreciative of all the concern*, I wrote in my journal.

Joe, meanwhile, continued to limit his contact with the outside world. Except for his nightly chats with Becky, occasional conversations with fellow leukemia patients Mary and John, and infrequent calls to his mother and sister, all of which he found exhausting, Joe kept his phone turned off. On those rare days when he seemed strong enough to handle distraction, I would slip out of the room and phone one of his friends to say, "Now is a good time to call." I tapped only those friends who could be counted on to make Joe laugh. Usually, I got the timing right. But not always. "Don't tell people to call, Wease," he scolded one afternoon after hanging up from a conversation, completely drained.

During those weeks when he was home between chemo rounds to rebuild his strength, his collisions with people's interest as he shuffled around the block usually left him less than inspired. After a neighbor would halt his labored progress to fill his ear with a story about some aunt who'd survived breast cancer, Joe would grouse, "How is that supposed to help?" If the cancer wasn't AML, the anecdote was meaningless. So was the "I know you're gonna lick this" fairy dust that people sprinkled along his path. But where Joe continued to hear advance obit material in people's cheerleading comments, I—

> *Jill! [Neighbor hurries across street to my driveway] We heard about Joe. This must be such a shock. I mean, Joe, he's so athletic and healthy . . . Well, you know what I mean. I always see him riding his bike. It's leukemia, right?*
>
> *[My dog claws neighbor's knees] Misty, knock it off. Sorry. She needs to go for a walk.*
>
> *You know, my husband's cousin had prostate cancer a few years ago. He's about the same age as Joe, and . . .Wait, how old is Joe?*
>
> *Sixty-four.*
>
> *Really? He looks much younger. This cousin is about twenty years younger. Anyway, he had prostate cancer and he's fine now.*
>
> *That's great. Um, I've got to walk Misty before I head into the city.*
>
> *Okay. Please tell Joe I was asking for him.*

Shit, where was I? Oh, right. I tended to hear a different subtext than Wease. To my mind, Joe and I were now Rorschach blots. People had only to look at one of us to project into our situation and wonder how they would cope. "How did you find out about Joe's leukemia?" (When was my last physical?) "Do the doctors

know how he got it?" (What should I avoid?) "What were his symptoms?" (Do I have any of them?) "How old is Joe, exactly?" (Phew,
I'm younger.) "How is Becky holding up?" (Would my kids freak
out?) "How many hours do you spend each day with Joe?" (*Eight?*
I'd lose my mind.) "Are you getting any sleep?" (Would I?) "Joe's
always been so fit." (If this could happen to him, what hope is there
for any of us?) "I just know he's going to beat this." (Cancer is beatable, right? It *has* to be beatable.)

If that didn't end the exchange, one of these three lines probably
did: "Don't hesitate to call if you need anything." "Joe is so lucky to
have you." "Tell Joe I'm praying for him."

Of the many well-intended expressions of concern, that last was
the one that left Joe and me feeling most awkward. We came to
our marriage from different religious upbringings. Joe was raised
Episcopalian, altar boy duties mandatory, except those Sundays
when his parents would load the kids into the car to take their
prize-winning Dalmatians to a dog show. I was raised Jewish,
Hebrew school mandatory, except those weekends when my parents would load the kids into the car to ski in Vermont. By the time
Joe and I met, we'd both long since landed in the same place on
organized religion: participation limited to annual holiday gatherings (Christmas, Passover) that involved family. We had some
differences on the spiritual front. (I believe in an afterlife; Joe did
not.) But neither of us felt inclined to debate, defend, or press our
position. Beliefs, we both felt, were just that: beliefs.

We did, however, share a non-God-centric view of life. When
things happened (for better or worse) and when they didn't (for
better or worse), it did not occur to either of us to credit, blame, or
even think about God. The arrival of leukemia in our lives did not
change that. As a result, we did not feel abandoned or punished by
an omnipotent being. (Where are You?) We did not believe that
if we thought the right thoughts, God would spare us. (She will

answer my prayers.) We did not think that God was watching and would intervene with a spirit of mercy. (He won't give me more than I can handle.)

As best I know, Joe did not pray. I, by contrast, have a flimsy habit of prayer, a holdover from the religious training of my youth that has evolved into an inconsistent practice of directing wishes for loved ones and thanks for positive developments in my life at an inchoate target. I have no clear idea Whom or What I am addressing; I have no expectation that I will be heard or answered. *I pray a lot of nights, Please, please, please. Who else am I going to beg?* I never told Joe about these silent cries for help; for me, prayer is a private matter.

Now, not only friends with whom Joe and I had never discussed religion, but also people we barely knew were thrusting their personal beliefs at us. For the first time, Joe and I heard about "prayer chains," as people of every denomination told us that Joe's name had been added to a list at a church, at a synagogue, or on the Internet. Was "Thank you" the proper response? We found the whole thing uncomfortable.

One Saturday, Becky returned from a friend's bar mitzvah and told me, "This really weird thing happened." During the service, the rabbi had asked the congregation to pray for some people who were sick, then rattled off a list of names. Becky, who'd told only her closest friends about her dad's illness, was startled to hear Joe's name among them. Cocooned in the self-absorbed bubble that is synonymous with adolescence—a bubble that served as a wonderful shield for Becky during this difficult period—it had not occurred to her that word might spread. When heads swiveled in her direction, she didn't like the attention.

That day as I ached for my child's discomfort, I thought I understood my unease with the frequent talk of prayer. It felt like a breach of privacy, both for the person who sent out the prayer and the person who was its intended target. Years later, I came across a line in Ann Patchett's memoir, *Truth and Beauty*, that for me captured far better the peculiar burden of other people's prayers: "What is prayer but a kind of worry?"

One week after Joe's diagnosis, I returned to work. When I first began at *People* in 1999, Joe was there, too, a corner office guy whose name was third from the top of the masthead. Though he'd left the magazine in 2003, there was still considerable affection for Joe among the editors, writers, researchers, and correspondents who remained—as I was reminded within seconds of unlocking my office door.

"Oh, my God, I heard about Joe." Ben, a fellow writer and one of my favorite office pals, dropped onto my couch and leaned toward me, his face contorted with pain. "What's going on?"

I adore Ben. There was no way I could avoid this conversation. But as I felt energy drain out of me, I realized this conversation was going to happen again and again if I didn't find a way to head people off. So many of my colleagues had a relationship with Joe; each would want a detailed accounting. When Ben circled around to, "If there's anything I can do," I seized the opportunity. Would he be willing to field questions? I could put him on the Weasel Update list, then point people his way. "Of course," he said.

Later that day, I sent an e-mail to the entire editorial staff, among them far-flung reporters Joe had overseen as chief of correspondents and people he'd hired when he was executive editor. "Hi, Everyone," I wrote. "I know word is out that Joe Treen has leukemia, and that there is a lot of shock and concern, as well as a lot of questions." For questions about AML, I directed them to the National Marrow Donor Program site. For the questions about what they could do, I provided my personal e-mail address and asked that they send messages to Joe. "As for his progress," I concluded, "I'll keep Ben updated if you want to know how Joe is doing. Thanks for all your good thoughts. jill" While I meant the note to be respectful and helpful, I also intended it to signal my preference that colleagues knock on Ben's door rather than—

> *[Knock, knock] Hi, how's Joe?*
> *[Jump, startled, turn from computer screen] Oh, hi. He's good, thanks.*
> *I can't get him off my mind. This must be so hard on Becky.*
> *She's holding up amazingly well.*
> *Remember all those pictures Joe had of her in his office? They covered a whole wall.*

Grrr. On this morning, as on most of the Mondays and Fridays that would follow, I had visited Joe before heading to the office. On this morning, as on most of the Mondays and Fridays that would follow, he'd expressed a wish that I could stay. Leaving him had been difficult, and it wouldn't get easier in the months ahead (though it could feel a hell of a lot harder when his blood counts and mood were bottoming out). To move my thoughts away from Joe and into the writing zone required an effort. When colleagues dropped by my office or stopped me in the hall, the coffee pantry, even the ladies' room, for a quick "How's Joe?" exchange, it shattered my concentration.

One of the few people who could empathize was Hannah, a colleague who'd lost her husband two years earlier after nursing him for several years. My memory of her visit to my office after Joe's diagnosis is visual: her hand on my knee; sorrow, loneliness, and empathy in her eyes. Internally (though I hope not visibly), I recoiled. What if widowhood was contagious? I suspect Hannah understood. As she rose to leave, she said, "Don't hesitate to call if you feel like talking." I never took her up on her offer; she never inquired about Joe again.

Wease and Becky apart, my colleagues were the people with whom I spent the most time during Joe's hospitalizations. Their concern and support never waned. Those at the upper reaches of the magazine told me to "take all the time" I needed, and let me know in advance of a round of layoffs that my job was not on the line. My immediate editors let me schedule vacation days on short notice and insisted that I "Go!" on those infrequent occasions when there was a medical emergency. Friends in the research library tracked down obscure articles about leukemia. Two of Joe's pals filled a mini-iPod with comedy sketches; two editors filled my refrigerator with enough food to feed Becky and me for a week. Most important, colleagues kept up a steady stream of e-mails to Joe, sharing memories of how he'd hired them, helped them, mentored them. Those messages touched Joe deeply. They touched me deeply, too.

Still, as the weeks stretched into months, what I needed more than anything from *People* (apart from my health-care benefits, which were covering Joe's treatment) was the distraction of work. It was a relief to lose myself in an assignment, to focus on the threading of a narrative, to think about the people at the heart of a story as I grabbed a salad from a nearby deli.

[Crowded lunchtime elevator] Jill! How's Joe doing?
[Peer through the crush of people to locate the voice]
Oh, hey. Good, thanks.
How's he handling the chemo?
[Pointedly sweep the cramped space with my eyes]
Fine. [Offer tight smile. Drop eyes.]

If there's anything I can do, don't hesitate to call.
[Moves to door] Really, I mean it.

A few days later I had a similar encounter, yet it felt very differ-ent to me. As I stepped into a packed elevator, I nodded to Ned, a colleague who works on another floor. After I exited into the lobby, I felt someone touch my elbow and turned to find Ned. Stepping closer, he dropped his voice so only I could hear. "I wanted to ask you," he murmured. "How is Joe doing?"

I had to restrain myself from hugging this man. He hadn't, like so many others, simply popped the question at the moment it occurred to him. By waiting until we were out of earshot of other people, he signaled his understanding that though Joe's illness was public knowledge, it remained, for me, an intensely private matter.

One day, I phoned Elizabeth. Since spotting her in the Montclair parking lot, I'd seen her just once, maybe a year or two after our non-encounter. On that occasion, an outdoor party for her husband, who happily was showing promise of sustained recovery, I was still so appalled by my earlier tongue-tied behavior that when I saw her strolling across the lawn, I turned so she couldn't see my face.

"I was wondering if you'd have lunch with me," I said when Elizabeth came on the line. "There's something I want to ask you. But if, when we meet, you feel the matter is too personal and don't want to answer, I'll understand completely."

As we settled at a restaurant table, the vibe I picked up was one of curiosity. I described the day I'd seen her in the parking lot and how I'd frozen, uncertain how to proceed. "The reason I asked you to lunch is to ask you this: What response would you have preferred?"

"Well, for people I know, it was okay for them to come up to me," Elizabeth demurred.

"But I didn't know you, really," I said. "We'd had lunch once, and that was years earlier."

With that, Elizabeth opened up. "I didn't find comfort in people's interest," she said. Repeatedly, she described the attention as "exhausting." She particularly hated "the sad face" people pulled when they talked to her. (To illustrate, she tugged her mouth into a frown with two fingers.) She also hated when people referred to her husband's cancer as "the tragedy," a phrase she heard often. "It drove me crazy."

"How did you handle all that?" I asked.

"Part of me felt I had to match people's expectations. So, if I was having an okay day, I felt I had to play the part of the anxious spouse. As a result, you don't get to have a good day even if you're having one." At the same time, she ignored phone calls, e-mails, and letters (including, no doubt, Joe's and mine). "I felt I could be responsive to my husband and my kids, or responsive to the greater world, because that can be a total energy suck." Her kids, she said, had expected her to be herself. That was what had kept her steady.

As we parted, I felt reassured, even vindicated. Like me, Elizabeth had found the barrage of concern more draining than sustaining. Still, there were three noticeable differences. While Elizabeth felt obligated to meet people's expectations with a display of anxiety, I felt compelled to allay people's worry with upbeat responses. Where I saw myself as a Rorschach blot onto which people projected their darkest fears, Elizabeth thought people used her situation to gain perspective on their own lives. "So many people feel deadened," she said. "They liked feeling. They liked participating in an emotional event." Finally, Elizabeth thought that people walked away from her feeling better because the encounter had "made them feel a connection to another person." Me? I thought people walked away thinking, *Thank God I'm not her.*

In hindsight, I'm more struck by our differences than our similarities. Not only had each of us found the one-size-fits-all script ill-fitting, but it had rubbed us wrong in distinct and unpredictable ways—to my mind further evidence how mistaken we are to cling to the one-size-fits-all assumption that such attention is welcome and comforting.

5
LIFELINES

Paradoxically, as depleting as I found the nonstop interest, the barrage of concern also buffered me from despair. How could I think, *Life sucks*, when the same cancer that was perniciously causing Joe's cells to multiply was also inspiring such a proliferation of kindness? With so many good-hearted sentiments and offers coming at me from so many directions, it was impossible to sink into hopelessness or isolation.

Certainly, I had no illusion I could navigate this thing solo. Leukemia treatment is a marathon, not a sprint. I knew I'd need both logistical help with Becky and emotional support for myself. But before I could identify what would truly be useful, I needed to get acquainted with the rhythms and requirements of my new universe. Anticipating a need for the sorts of practical assistance that people often find stress-relieving in times of crisis, my Montclair Writers Group considerately drew up a roster, with two women "on call" each week to handle carpools, grocery runs, or anything else I might need. I couldn't bring myself to tap it. All of these women were juggling the demands of work, spouses, children, and households; to help me out, any one of them would have had to rearrange her own tight schedule. *I can't help feeling the imposition, though I know they want to help*, I wrote after the group handed me the schedule.

I also had little desire to be relieved of such tasks. "Family time"

no longer existed. "Work time," beyond my *People* days, had evaporated; my novel-in-progress had been shelved and was no longer
part of my thinking. "Reading time" was also gone, my concentration too spotty to handle anything longer than magazine articles,
and even those only intermittently. Movies? Theatre? Lunch dates?
There was no place for "leisure time" in a universe bounded by my
new, inflexible schedule: Montclair-to-Roosevelt five days a week;
Montclair-to-*People* two days a week; home-to-Becky seven nights
a week. If I let go of the A&P runs and trips to CVS, what would be
left in my life beyond cancer? *In truth, doing the normal things is
just fine by me: laundry, straightening up, errands when I can.*

As the months ticked by, I came to appreciate that these daily
chores were more than fine; they were necessary. Unlike Joe's illness, such undertakings were finite: beginning, middle, end. The
act of wrestling a tangle of unwashed laundry into neat stacks of
clean clothes answered a need to see a task through to completion.
Taking Misty for a walk and watching her chase ecstatically after a
squirrel reminded me there was more to life than chemo drips and
biopsies. Walking the grocery aisles forced my thoughts out of the
hospital and back into the home.

Not that I couldn't have used some help. I hadn't been wrong
that first night when I wrote, *What would be useful? People delivering meals.* Under the best of circumstances, I don't enjoy cooking. Now, though, people's generosity was itself a peculiar kind of
burden. Unaware there were websites where people could sign up
for specific meals, and systems for leaving prepared food in coolers
on back porches, my thoughts about how a meal rotation might
work conjured only knots. "Let me know what time you'll be home
and I'll drop off a hot meal," someone might say. But how could
I commit to a time? Dire illness is a minute-to-minute business,
incompatible with people's daily planners. What if I made it home,
but wasn't hungry? The thought of a friend making time in her

busy schedule to cook a meal that didn't get eaten was more than I could deal with. For me, it was more palatable to eat dry cereal.

The idea of setting up a carpool for Becky was no less problematic. Any parent of a young teenager knows that the old adage about God applies to kids, as well: You make plans—your child laughs. If Becky wanted to hang with her friends uptown, how could I say for sure where she would be come pick-up time? How could I say for certain when some after-school activity would let out? The thought of a friend not finding my daughter where she was supposed to be, then sitting in her car waiting for Becky to show up (while her own children might need carpooling elsewhere), was an anxiety I preferred not to take on.

Moot point, anyway. While Becky understood that life was no longer normal, she wanted it to remain as recognizable as possible. She didn't want to climb into a stranger's car; she didn't want an unfamiliar adult in the house on nights when I was detained at the hospital. Who could blame her? Becky's life was in upheaval, too. So, red-faced, I reached out repeatedly to her former babysitter, Gay, and her closest friends' parents, some of whom I barely knew. Can Becky stay until 8:00, though it's a school night? Can she sleep over Saturday night? Month after month, none of them said no or made me feel like the burden I knew I was.

The same was true of my next-door neighbors, whom I leaned on again and again to let Misty in and out of the yard. At one point, I e-mailed a request that began, "Really sorry to be such a pain the butt," and got a prompt response: "You are never a pain in the butt!!!" I was as grateful for the forgiving sentiment as I was for the help. How could my requests not be a pain in the butt? This family doesn't even have a pet.

Later, friends would say, "It was hard. You're so used to being independent." But there was more to my resistance than an independent streak or discomfort about imposing. The cacophony of offers was a constant reminder that when people looked at me, they saw That Woman. While I was far too preoccupied by Joe's health to care how anyone regarded me, I was deeply concerned with how I regarded myself. If I was going to be steady for Joe and Becky, I needed to steer clear of this alien role people expected me to play and remain a person I recognized.

At fifty-one, I'd ridden enough emotional roller coasters to know that my most effective strategy for coping with adversity is to talk candidly about my upset with a small number of people whom I trust to safeguard my confidences. Given the magnitude of Joe's health crisis, my need for perspective was keener than ever. Given its public nature, my need for a zone of privacy was also more acute. But at the end of a long hospital day, I lacked the energy and desire to repeatedly detail Joe's progress and my distress. So, the members of my SWAT team, which clicked into place rapidly, each answered different needs. For discussions about Joe's medical treatment, I spoke nightly with my father. For matters concerning Becky and family, I spoke a few times a week with my sister, Ann. For conversations that helped me express and process my emotional turmoil, I spoke each evening with my friend Lynn.

The surprise in that lineup was my dad, whom I usually talked to three, four times a week. Though he'd never been my go-to guy for emotional stuff, I now phoned him each night to discuss the day's medical developments. My father, I knew, was a good listener and a reliable communicator; I could count on him to relay the details (often more complicated and sometimes more dire than what I put in the Update) to my mother and siblings without spin or distortion. As the weeks passed, I realized I'd come to rely on Dad as my medical sounding board. He never tried to steer my thinking; rather, he helped steer me back to information I'd given him earlier that might help inform whatever decision Joe and I were facing.

As for Ann, she anticipated I would resist her help (no doubt because she, too, had a great resistance to feeling like she was imposing on others) and navigated my balkiness brilliantly. That first visit when she'd done an end run around debate by simply showing up, she'd repeatedly demonstrated that my New Normal would be more manageable if I accepted her help. In addition to entertaining my daughter, mesmerizing my dog, and taking charge of my household, Ann had commandeered my plan to take Becky into the city for a brief visit with Joe, drive her back to Montclair, then return to the hospital. Instead, Ann had made the round-trip, leaving me more time with Joe and free of worry about Becky. If seeing Daddy in a hospital upset her, I knew Aunt Pooz would handle it.

With each subsequent visit, Ann weakened my resistance until she had me where she wanted: able to lean on her without feeling like a burden. During Joe's six months of hospitalizations, she came to Montclair five times to spend weekends with Becky. On a sixth trip, Ann made the five-hour drive south, loaded Becky, one of her friends, and Misty into the car, then whisked them away to Vermont for Becky's weeklong spring break. The girls had a blast; I had seven days to focus exclusively on Joe. It was an incredible gift.

That Ann got through to me where others couldn't owes much to the special chemistry that ferments over decades between sisters. I trusted that Ann's desire to lighten my load outweighed the aggravations of inconvenience; I accepted that for this limited period, helping me was her priority. I'd experienced that same strong desire to be of use a few years earlier when one of Ann's children was hospitalized. Back then, Pooz was living in Oregon, a distance that over fourteen years not only had curbed our time together, but also had eroded our intimacy. From a continent away, she insisted that she didn't want any family member to fly out; that having a guest in the house would only lend to her stress. No longer familiar with the rhythms of her daily life, but able to imagine feeling much the same way, I took Ann at her word. Looking back, I wish to hell I'd gotten on a plane and just showed up. I could have given Pooz a hug before she sent me packing—though I doubt she would have. Her dog, after all, needed walking, too.

For my inner life, my trusted keeper was Lynn. Way back during our first week of college, we'd discovered a mutual passion for writing. We'd been sharing our writing, our confidences, and our lives ever since. En route to becoming a clinical psychologist and a novelist, Lynn had acquired a formidable number of postgraduate degrees, but to me all that certification was redundant. As long as I've known Lynn, she's been a sympathetic listener, probing questioner, and insightful analyst.

That made for a peculiar problem now. After a long hospital day, I wanted neither to dig deep nor to have my emotional pulse taken. Mostly, I didn't want to talk at all. When I got home at night, I just wanted to spend time with Becky, then veg out in front of some sitcom until my eyes began to close. If the phone rang, I'd check caller ID to see if it was a member of Joe's or my family. All of them knew I was tired and uneager to talk; if any one of them was calling, there was a reason. Otherwise, I let the call go to voice mail to be dealt at a time when I thought I could avoid conversation by leaving a message. The one exception was Lynn, who I knew was thinking and worrying about me. She was too precious to me, our friendship too valuable, to not acknowledge her concern.

But we had a very different sense of what our nightly chats should be. Lynn would launch in with questions about Joe's medical condition and treatment. I'd try to redirect the conversation, asking about her kids, her life, her novel-in-progress. Lynn would offer a brief answer, then sweetly but firmly circle back to more questions. Often, I'd get off the phone agitated, thinking I'd let her next call go to voice mail. But I never did, in part because she'd shown me early on that she had practical as well as emotional support to offer. A cryptic notation in my reporter's notebook shortly after Joe's diagnosis indicates that Lynn raised questions I hadn't considered: *Disability Insurance? Time-Warner? Family Leave? Sabbatical?* A few days after she offered to look into Social Security for me, she supplied a packet of information that yielded an unexpected and timely treasure: not only could Joe tap into Social Security, but Becky was eligible for children's benefits, as well.

More important, there were things I could say to Lynn that I couldn't or wouldn't say to anyone else, knowing she could handle my fears, worry, and upset without making them her own. She was my repository for thoughts I needed to express, but didn't want to dwell on, wary that if I allowed them to dominate my thinking, depression might set in. On those rare occasions when Becky was away, Lynn also offered sanctuary in her Manhattan apartment, sparing me the commute and plying me with healthy meals. As her husband and two sons went about their evenings, the sounds of intact family life always provided a lift.

But, oy, those nightly questions. At times I wondered why I put up with Lynn's interrogations; other times I wondered why she put up with my bristly responses. I see now that Lynn was not only a safe repository for my emotions; she was a tolerant repository for my frustration at the relentless curiosity about Joe's health. Sometimes after one of her grillings, I'd say, "You should have been a reporter," and she'd laugh modestly, not grasping that I didn't mean it as a compliment. *She can't really believe that, yes, I want to discuss her novel. That, no, I don't want to talk about Joe's numbers, how he's doing, how I'm doing.* Nine months on, Lynn and her family traveled to Spain. Upon her return, I pressed for details about their trip. The next day, she told me, her tone anguished, "I feel so guilty." Guilty about what? "Going on and on about my vacation like that when you can't go away."

"Lynn, stop it."

"No, really. It was inconsiderate."

"Lynn! I wanted to hear about your vacation!"

Unlike Ann, Lynn never experienced the lens shift that would enable her to view my situation through my eyes. I was lucky she didn't. Because of her tenacity, she was able at a critical juncture in Joe's care to connect me with an oncology specialist—at 11:00 at night. And because of her intimate acquaintance with, and sometimes better memory of, the unfolding drama in my life, she was able to enlarge my perspective at difficult moments. Later, when time and distance enabled us to talk about our dynamic throughout Joe's illness, Lynn told me that she'd mined for detail because she thought of herself as my "backup brain."

"You were!" I said, delighted. And with that, my own lens shifted.

What I encountered with Lynn was an extreme version of what I faced pretty much every time I stepped out of my house. People didn't understand my need was to enter their worlds, not for them to enter mine. It took a while to identify the friends who heard me when I said I'd rather talk about something else; who could continue to share the challenges in their own lives without feeling they were burdening me; who could make me laugh; who could see beyond the wife of a sick man to engage the writer, the parent, the daughter, the interested friend, the news junkie, the cultural consumer. These people, some of them casual friends at the outset, became my lifelines.

The first to signal that she still saw a three-dimensional human being was my Montclair friend Pamela, a fellow magazine writer with whom I'd shared monthly lunches for years. Sure, we talked about what our kids and husbands were up to, but mostly we discussed what we were working on, what we were reading, what issues were roiling the journalism world. After Joe's diagnosis, I began to get brief daily e-mails from Pamela advising me of her availability for errands or anything else I might need. She didn't push. She also didn't take no for an answer. Okay, if not dinner tonight, then when? If not this movie, which one? Often her messages included the reminder, "Breathe. In. Out. In. Out." When we were able to get together, we talked about the sorts of things we always had. Sometimes Pamela would ask if I was thinking about finishing the novel I'd been working on for two years before Joe got sick. I wasn't. But I loved that she assumed me capable of the effort and thought it important to keep the writer in me alive.

As our friendship deepened, Pamela began to join Becky and me for occasional dinners. It was never a planned event that might leave me stressing about getting home at a designated hour. Instead, the phone would ring as I was leaving the hospital or as I walked through the kitchen door. "Hey. It's Pamela. I was at the farmer's market today and have too much salad. You up for dinner?" Then she'd show up with pretty much all the fixings for a meal, act like my paltry contribution of wine was most excellent, and distract me with conversation while she cooked. Over dinner, she'd engage Becky in animated discussion about films and rock bands. Afterwards, she never stayed long, always pleading work. It was a canny seduction. Becky grew so comfortable with Pamela that it became okay for Pamela to handle the occasional carpool; I grew so comfortable with Pamela that I found I could ask such favors without feeling like an annoying drag on her time. Hers was the number I dialed at 4:00 a.m. when I suddenly needed an adult to come stay with Becky while I drove Joe to the emergency room.

In April 2008, ten months after what we thought was Joe's final hospitalization, Wease landed back in the transplant ward with complications. One day, my cell phone rang. "Just checking in," Pamela said. "How's Joe doing?"

"Are you okay?" I said.

"Why do you ask?"

"I don't know. You sound funny."

There was a silence. Then she said, "Jack told me he wants a divorce."

Thirty-six years of marriage. Gone. Just like that.

I doubt Pamela had intended to share her news when she dialed my number, but my question had caught her vulnerable and off-guard. Even so, she could have retreated, insisting I had enough to worry about. Instead, Pamela gave me a valuable gift: she let me be a friend. Now, I was the one checking in to see how *she* was doing, pushing impromptu dinners, pressing her to come to Pennsylvania with Joe and me on weekends.

Over the next three months (a period when she would tell no one else, not wanting the sympathy, the gawking, or the attention), we talked about Pamela's pain and we talked about Joe's recuperation. Of course we did. But we also talked about our writing assignments, her teaching, our professional goals. One Saturday while chatting on the patio in Pennsylvania, I made noises about feeling ready to find a writing project now that Joe was back on the mend. Pamela got right on top of it, talking ideas and encouraging me. That gave rise to my first non-*People* piece of writing in more than a year, an essay about the "before and after" of Joe's diagnosis, which Pamela edited down to size, then helped me place with *The Washington Post Magazine*. At the time, it felt like an enormous accomplishment.

Over the months other friends emerged who could be counted on to stimulate my brain cells and replenish my spirit. Most of them belonged to the Montclair Writers Group that a friend and I had started in 1997 after we both traded magazine jobs for self-employment. Back then, our aim had been to create a network of freelance journalists who would share information, advice, and contacts. As novelists and essayists joined, our discussions broadened; as affection and trust deepened, our monthly meetings grew more personal. Through the years, we'd offered emotional support to members grappling with difficult issues: breast cancer, the death of a parent, a child's learning disability, divorce.

Yet I delayed putting out word to the group about Joe's diagnosis, uneager to face the phone calls and pained looks that I knew would greet me at every turn once word got out. About two weeks after Joe checked into Roosevelt, I finally told a group member. "Is there anything I can do?" she asked. "Yes," I said. "Tell the group at the next meeting, but please ask them not to call me right now." The group promptly drew up that schedule of errand-runners, and, respectful of my request not to phone, e-mailed a request to be added to the Weasel Update chain. Then, various members began sending notes of encouragement to Joe and wonderfully supportive messages to me.

When I was able to rejoin the group during a lull between chemo rounds, they blew right past my vague explanation of why I hadn't tapped their roster to focus on what I needed *now*. With Joe home, was I up for lunches? Movie outings? "I'd welcome your company," I said. But not lunches. What I craved was exercise. If anyone was up for an early-morning jaunt around Brookdale Park, "I'd love to walk and talk, but not about Joe."

Thus began my morning walks, two, three days a week that I came to count on for distraction, stimulation, and rejuvenation. The first person to come into more vivid focus was Nora. Through the winter, rare was the morning I didn't find an uplifting e-mail from Nora waiting in my inbox. She had a gift for saying what I needed to hear. ("What a great spirit and sense of adventure and humor you manage to convey in your weasel updates. They are a gift to your family and friends and I hope they are a tonic to you to write.") She also had a tenacious determination to help. ("I'd be happy to drop off anything you need on your doorstep and then disappear...") Ignoring that I kept ignoring her offers, Nora continued to offer her help.

During our loops around the park, we discovered that our mothers were a mutual hot button. Nora had withstood many daughterly worries and frustrations in the years before her mother's death; she could empathize with my worry and frustration about my own mother's deteriorating health. As our conversations grew more intimate, I came to understand why Nora was so sensitive to my situation, not only with my mother, but with Joe as well. She'd been through several prolonged illnesses in her own family; she knew that worry doesn't let up, no matter how many days or months tick by.

Along that same two-mile park loop, other relationships deepened. I learned about friends' struggles with their children and parents, their teaching and writing. In May 2007, Celeste waited patiently, as she always did, until we were unleashing our dogs at walk's end, to say, "I know you don't want to talk about it, but just tell me real quick, how's Joe?" After my brief response, she said, as she always did, "Well, if there's anything I can do, you only have to ask."

"There is," I said, surprising both of us.

My sister-in-law, Esme, would soon be arriving from California to donate blood for Joe's stem cell transplant. For her, preparation involved two weeks of daily injections of a white blood cell booster that Joe's doctors wanted to monitor. For me, that meant sixteen days with a guest in my house at a time when Joe would be crashing from pre-transplant chemo. The prospect of juggling host obligations with caregiving duties was stressing me out. "Do you think the group could provide dinners for those two weeks?" I asked.

A few hours later, Celeste messaged, "Within 15 minutes of e-mailing the group about dinner, there's only one day left untaken and at this rate, that won't be true by the time you read this." Five days after that, she sent a list of names and dates, and this: "You have a lineup of dinners coming to you, including on the weekend— hope that's okay, but so many people wanted to do it, I thought, couldn't hurt to have a little extra."

Through misted eyes, I wrote to the group. "I haven't gotten teary much these last several months, but I'm a bit dewy-eyed right now. You guys are amazing. AMAZING!" Thanks to them, Esme's visit proved more manageable than I anticipated (and the meals more savory than Esme had reason to hope).

In time, I would thank each of my walking partners for heeding my appeal for conversation that didn't focus on illness—and, later, death and dying. Always, the response was pretty much the same: "You were so clear about what you needed. It took the guesswork out of it and made it easy to help you." That sentiment reinforced what my sister had said to me right at the start: "I can't know what you need unless you tell me."

Toward that end, websites that match volunteers with specific requests—a meal, a child's carpool, a ride to a doctor's appointment—can be enormously helpful. Friends have the satisfaction of knowing they're answering a real need. Caregivers gain precious time and avoid the sorts of planning conversations that can sound so draining to weary ears. ("I'll take the Tuesday carpool. No, wait.

Sorry. My daughter has a dance recital rehearsal that day and she really wants me to be there. Can I do it Wednesday?...Oh. How about Thursday? I'm good up until 4:00, but then my son has—") When I recently told a friend that I didn't learn about such sites until weeks into Joe's treatment, she said, her tone shocked, "No one offered to organize that for you?" I assured her I would have said no, anyway. But her comment made me realize that getting such a network up and running for a harried caregiver can be a gift unto itself.

Still, a grid of tasks answers only logistical needs, not emotional ones. Experience has convinced me that when people offer "anything," many have a genuine desire to provide support that is truly helpful. But people are not mind readers; they need and appreciate guidance.

Despite my resistance, people's good intentions and kindness *did* get through. While I found the individual expressions of concern wearying, they provided a surround sound of support that was tremendously comforting. Some people even managed to penetrate my stubborn resistance and offer just the right sentiment at a tender moment. During Joe's transplant, for instance, a response to an Update, forwarded by Esme from a friend of hers I'd never met, moved me to tears: "She sure does love the guy." During an interval when I was feeling overwhelmed by so much family illness, a friend's casual, "You're the sturdiest person I know" provided just the bolstering I needed. And a good shot of humor could always make me feel better. After Joe put out an e-mail saying he was handling the day's Update because the toll of a late *People* close, a basement flood, and a sick husband had made me "soft and lazy" and in need of a nap, a far-flung friend fired back, "Dump the bitch!"

Joe's six months of hospitalizations have settled in my memory much as I experienced them at the time: a blur of largely indistinguishable days. Yet six years later, countless acts of kindness continue to shine through that haze, undated, but unforgotten. A sampling:

- The neighbor who shoveled my sidewalk on a snowy morning before I woke up.
- The couple who drove three hours round-trip to take Becky for a weekend.
- The next-door caterer who asked if I'd like some of her fresh-made soup, then banked my response that my freezer was currently full, but I'd love soup sometime up the road. Weeks later, she showed up at my kitchen door with an armload of containers. When I returned them empty, she quickly reappeared with new ones, a gift she continued to supply throughout the winter.
- The friend who, understanding that lunches in Montclair were a no-go for me, interrupted her writing day to schlep into the city and provide an entertaining meal on a boring hospital day.
- The friend who asked what she could do, then didn't shrug off as inconsequential my answer, "Keep playing Wordscraper with me." After that, she always made sure we had three games going.
- The owner of a local carpet store who rearranged his service roster when, post-transplant, Joe was unexpectedly offered an early release from the hospital, but couldn't come home until all our rugs were disinfected.
- The West Coast college friend who heard me when I said, "Call more often. I'm going out of my mind to talk about anything but Joe." One, two times a week, he'd phone

and we'd dissect the political landscape, compare our
workout regimens, crack each other up with stories about
our teenage daughters. "We're laughing *with* them, not *at*
them," we'd guiltily remind each other—then crack up
all over again.

- The friend who, upon learning that Joe was considering
a stem cell transplant, phoned to tell me about a friend
of hers who had recently undergone the procedure and
was recovering nicely. After Joe's transplant two months
later, I asked how her friend was doing. "Okay, full dis-
closure," she said. "She died just as Joe was going into the
hospital for his transplant." Her sensitivity touched me,
but didn't surprise. This friend had been through treatment for breast cancer; she understood the importance
of timing.

So did Dr. B, who throughout Joe's months of chemo had steered
us away from discussions that got ahead of what was unfolding.
When the question of a stem cell transplant finally came due, Joe
was facing rectal surgery to repair gastrointestinal damage so painful that he couldn't focus on the medical debate erupting around
us. Though he'd been in remission since the conclusion of his first
chemo round, the four-member transplant team at Mount Sinai
Hospital, citing irregularities in Joe's cells, was insistent he was at
risk of relapse and needed a transplant immediately; Dr. B., arguing
that the same irregularities had existed prior to treatment, favored
a fourth round of chemo. When I sought a third opinion, I got this
expensive piece of fence-straddling: "A transplant may not work,
but it's pretty clear that some people do very, very well following
this procedure." That doctor's "may not work" had a chilling name

in the medical literature I was consuming on a crash-course basis: transplant-related mortality.

Emotionally, I was in the worst place I'd been since Joe's diagnosis. *I'm thinking I'm going to lose Joe if we don't do this transplant, but that the transplant risks losing him even sooner . . .Yesterday I learned that [a former colleague's] husband unexpectedly dropped dead of a heart attack at 65. It reminds me that I'm fortunate in having time to brace for this, though there is no bracing; to prepare, though there is no preparing; to rehearse, though there is no real rehearsal. At best, I can steel myself for an unthinkable prospect that I now can't stop thinking about.*

It was in this frame of mind that I approached Dr. B, alone at the nurses' station one evening, and asked about Joe's prospects.

"With no transplant," she said carefully, "I would be extremely and pleasantly surprised if he were doing well after two years."

Struggling against the sinking sensation in my chest, I said, "I didn't grasp until now how limited his time might be."

"We tend to get lulled by treatment," she said. Taking things a step at a time through the chemo had been a good approach, she continued. The alternative now being suggested by the Mount Sinai team "would have been too much to consider before."

She was probably right. But the time had arrived for forthright discussion. "If it were your husband," I said, "what would you do?"

Dr. B's facial expression softened and suddenly the divide between us melted away. We were two wives discussing a hideous decision. "I honestly don't know," she said. "I probably would want to know the mortality rate. If acceptable, I would consider it." I responded with the findings from a new study of older patients that I'd discovered. After expressing surprise at the encouraging results, Dr. B shifted into a different gear. "Another way to think of transplant is this: a patient will either live longer and some of it will be high-quality or the patient won't live longer and will have a lousy quality of life." She paused. "There's also this way to think of it. Consider the worst-case scenario and then ask yourself if you would regret that you hadn't done everything possible."

There it was, the answer I needed. There was no predicting the outcome of a transplant, particularly in a patient Joe's age. But in a few weeks, Becky would turn thirteen. If Joe and I didn't do everything possible to keep him in her life, let alone mine, there was one thing I *could* predict: if worst came to worst, I would have enormous regrets.

There is one more moment I want to share, a quiet gesture that stands out as the most selfless act of giving I've ever witnessed. Maybe because it played out at a time when I was reeling and vulnerable, or maybe because it emerged from a history rich with context and meaning, this act of kindness touched me more deeply than any other. I'm referring to the phone call that had prompted my college friend Richard to contact me two days after Joe's diagnosis, the one placed by my brother Jonathan.

At the time, my overriding need was for information that would help me understand what Joe and I were up against. Jonathan understood this about me—which, in hindsight, I find remarkable. In 2003 when Jonathan had experienced his own life-shattering crisis, the unexpected dissolution of his twenty-year marriage, his most acute need had been to vent his anger and upset, and talk about his confusion and fears. Nightly for almost two years, I'd provided that ear for him. It would have been natural for Jonathan to reach into his own experience and surmise that I required the same kind of support. Instead, Jonathan had listened carefully when I told him (for the second time, to his embarrassment) about Joe's diagnosis, hearing in my stream of words how aggressively

I'd been gathering information about leukemia and its treatment. When he hung up, he apparently came to two conclusions: my own fears and challenges, as distinct from Joe's, were getting short shrift; and there was nothing in his own experience he could draw on to meet that need.

So Jonathan did something subtle and complicated: he stepped outside of himself. With egoless grace, he turned his thoughts to identifying someone whose counsel might truly be of use. I don't know what pathways Jonathan's mind traveled from there, but the course of action he arrived at was to call the Harvard Law School switchboard and track down a stranger he knew I admired, one who, he remembered from our conversation a month earlier, had lost his wife. Jonathan's determination to step out of his own shoes and into mine was, in and of itself, remarkable. But to my mind, what boosted that gesture from considerate to extraordinary was the huge chunk of Jonathan's ego that could have stopped him from picking up the phone.

Just fifty weeks apart in age, my younger brother and I are so tight that back when he was deciding which college to attend, I placed a classified ad in our hometown newspaper: *Come to me, Meus.* Loving and well intentioned, my message proved to be misguided. Princeton was the wrong school for Jonathan. Early his freshman year, he got it into his head that he lacked the intellectual rigor of his fellow students. Over the next four years while Jonathan flourished on Princeton's playing fields and theater stages, he sat mute in his classes, constantly feeling diminished by what he perceived to be the greater intelligence of the people around him. Where my pantheon of academic gods totaled one (Richard), Jonathan's was populated by just about everybody on campus. Though he steadily earned Bs, he was convinced he was "faking it." When I'd try to shore up his confidence, he'd reply without any trace of resentment, "You belong here. I don't. If I had it to do over, I'd pick a different school." On the day he received his diploma, he joked—ha, ha—that he'd graduated "*summa cum difficulty.*"

Jonathan went on to become a successful executive-level software salesman. I've seen him seduce corporate, community, and religious audiences with his natural people skills, contagious enthusiasm, and sharp mind. My mother exaggerated only somewhat when she used to boast: "Jonathan could sell the zipper off a fly."

Still, cold-calling Richard? A man whose formidable intellect and academic achievements embody the essence of what makes Jonathan feel small to this day? That required a selflessness —not to mention a steely pair of balls—that amazed me. When I phoned my brother to thank him for contacting Richard, I asked, "Whatever made you think to call him?"

"He's been through something none of the rest of us have," Jonathan said. "I thought maybe talking to him would help you."

"Jesus, Meus. That was incredible of you. To bring up something so personal with someone you've never met, to explain my situation—"

"I didn't have to say much at all," Jonathan cut in. "Richard said he understood. He asked for your phone number. He said he'd take it from there."

I could all but see Jonathan shrugging his shoulders. He didn't regard what he'd done as a big deal. But I did, and I still do. My big-hearted brother, whose main takeaway from his elite education was that he processes information too slowly, thinks uncreatively, and has little intelligent to offer, had thrown me precisely the lifeline I needed. How? By rapidly synthesizing my fears, needs, and circumstance to come up with an outside-the-box course of action that never would have occurred to the sister he credits with having the smarts he's convinced he lacks.

Recently, I asked Jonathan if placing that call had been difficult for him, given Richard's prominent standing in an academic world he finds so daunting. "That call was easy for me," he said. "I was acting from my heart, not my brain."

6

CONTAGION

WHILE THE DECISION TO SIGN ON to a stem cell transplant had been agonizing, the procedure was unexpectedly simple—for Joe, that is. Though ground down by an intense bombardment of chemo, Wease approached T-Day in good spirits, scribbling a note for me to hand-deliver to Esme in the bowels of Mount Sinai Hospital: "Dear Baby Sister, don't fuck it up." Poor Esme, meanwhile, had to lie on her back for more than three hours, arms splayed at a right angle to her torso, squeezing a plastic ball to increase the flow of blood wending through tubes connected to a huge machine that harvested her white blood cells and fed the red ones and platelets back into her body. After some lab voodoo, the white blood cells arrived in Joe's room, our hope for a long, healthy future together packaged inelegantly in a small plastic bag.

"That's it?" I said, as a nurse strung the bag of colorless fluid on Joe's IV pole.

"I know," she said, laughing. "Most people find the actual transplant anticlimactic."

Me, I found it amazing.

The transplant doctors, in turn, found Joe amazing. Calling him their "perfect patient," they moved up his release date. After he returned home on June 22, 2007, he continued to astonish. His first day back in Montclair, he walked—well, hobbled—once around our block, me by his side anxiously monitoring his every step.

Within two weeks he was up to forty-minute solo jaunts. "This is the first time I feel good since the transplant," he told me in early August. By October, Joe was back at his desk working. His doctors felt he was doing so "superbly" that when he asked if he could fly to California in January for his mother's ninety-fifth birthday and book plane tickets for an April trip to Italy, they green-lighted both requests. Through that winter, all Becky could talk about was the gorgeous villa we'd rented with her godfathers and other friends; the incredible meals we were going to eat; the beautiful places we were going to visit. Joe and I were excited, too. Tuscany was going to be our quiet victory lap.

One day I walked into Joe's home office. When he turned from his computer with his please-don't-bother-me-Wease look, I rattled off whatever was on my mind and quickly backed out the door—then stopped short and stepped back in. "Hey, Wease. We didn't say, 'I love you.'" It took a second for Joe's distraction to clear and for my meaning to register. "I guess this means we must think you're getting better." Joe smiled. "Love you," I said.

"Love you," he said.

Two weeks before year's end, I sent out an e-mail: "Joe and I agree it's (happily) time to put the Weasel Update to rest. Happy Holidays to all." Our snail mail holiday cards had always pictured only Becky, but this year we felt we owed our friends an image that showed Joe on the mend. The resulting card was so joyous that I thought it was a damn masterpiece. On the front the message read: *In the immortal words of Crosby, Stills, Nash & Young . . .* Inside, there was a color photo of Joe sandwiched between Becky and me on a porch swing, Misty curled in Becky's lap, Joe smiling broadly and looking robust, his once-chemosized bald pate covered by a full head of hair. Under the happy family tableau were two words: *Carry On.*

Three months later, Joe reentered the hospital battling breathlessness. Over the next three weeks, he checked in and out of Mount Sinai two times as the transplant team tried to get a handle on his problem. The main suspect was graft-versus-host disease, a common post-transplant complication that involves the donor's cells attacking the recipient's organs and tissues. We were told, "A little chronic GVHD is a good thing," "We see this all the time," and "It can get completely better." We were also told, "If the GVHD is in the lungs, that's a potentially serious problem." As there was no way to know for sure (GVHD doesn't show up in a lung biopsy), doctors "deduced" GVHD in the lungs and began a steroid-driven course of treatment.

During these tense weeks, neither Joe nor I wanted to believe health issues were going to overrun our lives again. Reluctant to restart the Update, we confined news of his setback to family, a handful of friends, and colleagues affected by the disruption in our work schedules. My journal, the place where I've always vented and processed upset and worry, also remained inactive; the first eight months of 2008 show only two entries. The one that speaks of Joe's relapse (*Downright scary*) also mentions my parents' health, my sister's typically funky results on her annual mammogram, a brother's job problems, Pamela's suddenly collapsed marriage—a clear indication that my window on the world hadn't closed.

Our victory lap in ruins, Joe and I put Becky on a plane to Italy in mid-April to join our friends for the trip we'd all long-planned, then repaired to our house in Pennsylvania. We joked that while our daughter had Siena, we had Susquehanna; while Becky had the culinary delights of Tuscany, we had the many flavors of Jell-O, the one food Joe could tolerate. We indulged our gallows humor, wondering if Joe got a big advance for the book proposal he'd just completed, then croaked, would the advance have to be returned? *Such is life these days. Not fun. But not a disaster . . . hardest thing to face: this post-leukemia stuff isn't over.*

Or was it? On the second day of our vacation we drove north to visit a former *People* colleague who was guest teaching at Syracuse University. As we walked the sprawling campus, Joe showed every indication that he was rapidly putting the relapse behind. My hope resurged. The man was a completist; he would get through this.

I was less sanguine about my mother. For years she'd been suffering assorted aches, unconvincingly diagnosed as rheumatoid arthritis, which had taken such a hit on her physical strength that she now required a wheelchair. More recently, food had begun to make her dizzy, causing a dramatic drop in weight. Accustomed to an active life, Mom hated the whole business of aging. Repeatedly, she made clear she wanted no part of medicines, hospitals, or heroic measures. A believer in the afterlife, she was ready to move on.

Briefly, it seemed she might do just that. The day of our trip to Syracuse, Joe and I returned home to the unexpected news that my mother had suffered a mild heart attack. Over the next two weeks, Mom, cautioned by her physician that a second heart attack might follow, signed up for hospice home-care. Two weeks after that, she was back in Mom mode, wondering when Joe and I would visit. "We'll have some very interesting discussions when you come, given what different phases of life we're at," she said by phone. Citing Joe's parents' longevity, she said, "Joe has every reason to think he'll live to one hundred and twenty. But not me. I don't want that. Everybody makes their choices. There's no right or wrong."

Joe and I found the contrast between our mothers stark. Mine, at seventy-nine, was rooting for death to take its natural course. Short, at ninety-five, was battling so hard to hang onto life that when Joe suggested she consider hospice care, she shrieked, "You think I'm going to die!" then refused to talk to him for days. Though age was having a field day with Short—a heart attack; a brush with colon cancer; breathing problems—she refused to wear a device that would summon help if she needed it. Her stubbornness left Joe and his sister feeling frustrated and helpless.

My siblings and I felt the same way, but our main concern wasn't for our mother. While all four of us could accept that Mom wanted to go, none of us could accept the toll it was taking on our father. Uncharacteristically exhausted and dispirited as he cared for my mother round-the-clock, Dad was proving as intransigent as Short when it came to our pleas that he hire a home health-care worker. So we worried about him—and with good reason. Ann had watched her mother-in-law's health wane as she cared for a husband debilitated by Parkinson's disease; ultimately, she'd landed in the hospital with pancreatic cancer and preceded her husband to the grave. Jonathan had watched his mother-in-law's vitality ebb while she cared for a husband debilitated by Alzheimer's; after he died, her robustness never returned. Alan was now watching his father-in-law grow exhausted as he cared for a wife debilitated by myelodysplasia. I'd seen the same toll on my mother-in-law during the years she'd cared for a husband debilitated by the challenges of macular degeneration.

To give my father some relief, my sibs and I were rotating monthly visits to my parents in North Carolina. Alan, who lived closest, handled far more than his fair share. With Joe's relapse behind us, I was able to visit that August. The following month it was Ann's turn. On September 7, I called to get her update on the folks.

We chatted about Mom. We chatted about Dad. We must have been a good ten, fifteen minutes into our conversation when Ann said, "I have bad news." Then, without a pause or a change of inflection, she said, "I have cancer."

My head reared, as if I'd been slapped. Remembering her funky mammograms, I said, "Breast?"

"No. That's the weird thing. It's cancer of the colon. And I'm not even fifty."

I wish I had shouted, "Colon cancer, Pooz! Colon cancer!" But what came to mind was my mother-in-law's surgery at age ninety, following a stage 1 colon cancer diagnosis. Snip, snip. All gone. No muss, no fuss. No chemo, either. "It can be very uncomplicated," I said.

So calm. So voice-of-experience reasonable.

So incredibly full of bullshit. I hung up the phone and burst into tears.

Her next oncology appointment a week away, Ann sent an unambiguous signal that she did not want to be crowded by our concern. She would speak to my parents each day and let the family grapevine carry news of any developments to the rest of us, meaning her siblings and Gatha, the woman who'd helped raise the four of us. Beyond that, Ann was so averse to disruptions in her daily routine or anyone else's that she insisted she wanted no visits from siblings; planned not to tell her colleagues and friends about her diagnosis; wanted no family members on hand even when it came time for the surgery to excise the abdominal mass that had flagged her condition. My parents and brothers, pros at the art of restraint after dealing with me through Joe's treatment and recovery, knew what was required. I, though new to the role of spectator, knew what was required, too. Ann had role-modeled it, for God's sake: Get on her wavelength; don't assume her needs will be the same as mine.

Should have been a snap, given my intimate acquaintance with the peculiar burden of people's concern. I knew how unhelpful, even counterproductive, it could be to crowd Ann. Much as I wanted my sister right in front of me so I could take my own measure of her mood, I understood such access was now her husband's privilege, not mine. He and Ann would let me in as much or as little as they needed. I also empathized with Ann's desire to keep people at bay and not alarm or impose. I even knew from my mother-in-law's experience that Ann's treatment might involve no more than a single surgery. Though I'd been jolted by information on the Internet showing a single-digit survival rate for stage 4 colon cancer patients, there was considerable statistical evidence that Ann was twenty years too young to be a likely candidate for advanced-stage disease.

I knew, I knew, I knew. Yet for all that hard-earned knowledge, one critical piece had eluded me. My sister and those friends who'd given me the space to escape the obsession of worry had set their own concerns aside so gracefully that they'd made it look easy. Now, I was discovering just how challenging it really was. Though well-acquainted with Ann's penchant for charting her own course, I hungered for the more familiar film script, the one where, cast as dependable best friend, I got to attach myself to her side and offer my sturdy shoulder and sympathetic ear; lighten her worry with witty one-liners; wipe her tears. Daily, my finger itched to dial Ann's number. I wanted to hear the tone of her voice. I wanted firsthand updates about her husband and kids. I wanted to make sure she knew, just in case I hadn't made myself absolutely clear, "Anything, anything at all, I'm here for you." Daily, I had to remind myself, *This isn't about what you want; it's about what Ann needs.*

Most days, I heeded that inner voice, sending e-mails more

upbeat than I felt, which Ann could read or ignore. On those days, I dealt with my anxiety by phoning my parents or brothers to ask if they had any new read on Ann. But that was only most days. After I would phone Ann and suggest, yet again, that she'd need a watchdog in the hospital to run errands and keep an eye on her comfort and meds, I'd hang up with her fatigue and lack of enthusiasm for my unsought advice ringing in my ears. Worse than helpless, I felt unhelpful. *You of all people know better,* I'd berate myself. *Sit back. Shut up. Respect her wishes.*

Sometimes hard-earned knowledge really sucks.

After Ann's next medical appointment, she informed the family in a brief e-mail that her surgical oncologist had shed no new light on the extent of her cancer. He had, however, laid out his plan to go in laparoscopically on the abdominal mass, which was close to the surface, then, if need be, proceed to open surgery. The first OR opening, he'd told her, was a month from now.

One part of my brain reasoned, *A month? Well, then it's probably not so bad.* Another part yelped, *A month? That's insane!*

For hours, I debated whether to call. Finally, settling on the winning strategy adopted by my friends Nora and Pamela—make yourself available, but don't push—I dialed. "Hey, Pooz," I said. "Sorry for the call, but I can't *not* call." Ann laughed and detailed her follow-up meeting with the surgeon. We both snorted when she told me this was the third appointment at which he'd managed to avoid the word *cancer.* When I asked how the month-long delay before surgery was sitting with her, Ann signaled by a shift in tone and subject that she didn't want to discuss it. "I *did* think of something I could use," she said. As an early birthday gift from her sibs, she wanted a fully loaded iPod she could listen to, post-surgery.

She and her husband, Jim, also wanted to know if I'd consider writing daily updates to the family while Ann was in the hospital. Were they kidding? "Of course," I said.

As our conversation wound down, I said that I'd hesitated to call, not wanting to intrude. "You're kidding," Ann replied. Emboldened by her response, I said, "I'm going to check in each day, if that's all right. If you're not in the mood to talk, you'll let me know."

"Yes, call," she said. "I'll just tell you if I'm not up for it."

Three days later when I phoned to say a new, ready-to-play iPod was en route, Ann told me she'd spoken to an oncologist friend, who'd warned that putting off surgery for a month was "ridiculous," given the size of Ann's abdominal mass. To my relief, Ann was now pushing her surgeon to reschedule the procedure. I also spoke with Jim, who seemed receptive, even relieved, when I asked if I could check in with him occasionally. At one point, I mentioned how helpful I'd found it to take notes during consultations with doctors. That night Ann told me, with a forced laugh, "That's so you and Joe, wanting to prepare. We're more take-it-as-it-comes."

Noted.

Ann and I seem to be finding our footing so I can be of use to her, as she was to me . . . So different being not-the-main caretaker. Don't want to push, but want to make clear I'm available for anything . . . Mentioned to Dad my concern that Ann wanted to disappear into the hospital, alone. Asked him to press on her that she had to have someone along. A few days later, he told me they'd had that conversation and had told her, "Jill is very good at this sort of thing." He said she answered, "I know. She is." Doesn't mean she'll want me there; I get that. But want to be available . . . Let [my editor] know I might need to take off suddenly on a health issue. She thought, of course, it was Joe. I teared up. I am way too teary for talks like that.

Unlike with Joe, where my determination to be "strong" had left me dry-eyed, almost any thought of my sister turned me into a wet mess. *With Ann, because it's a bit removed—Joe's health/my well-being are inextricable—I can afford a bit of teariness.* I regarded my crying as more an expression of worry than fear. At forty-nine, Ann was a model of fitness: a swimmer, a skier, an avid hiker who'd once trekked the entire Appalachian Trail from Georgia to Maine. She was primed to rebound quickly from a surgery that her doctor clearly regarded as minor. He'd ignored her appeals to move up the date. He'd also ignored her appeals to track down the results of a pro forma CT scan. Five days later, those lab findings finally reached his desk.

Then everything changed. *The cancer has metastasized to her liver, aorta, and lymph nodes. Shocking. Stage 4 colon cancer.*

Abruptly, Ann's surgery was scheduled for the following morning. With it now clear that the procedure would involve major cutting, she accepted my offer to be her daytime watchdog; Jim, an architect with limited vacation time, would handle caregiving duties at night. During my five-hour drive to Vermont, I sobbed nonstop. *Surreal,* I kept thinking. *This is absolutely surreal.* Miles from her exit, I pulled into a rest stop to wash my face.

When I arrived at Ann's house, I found my sister carefully reviewing a hospital advance directive form to clarify for her husband which medical interventions she would accept, and which ones she wouldn't. "I don't want a compromised life," she kept saying. At her side, Jim sat silent, too stunned to say anything.

That night I asked Ann to let me tell her college friend Priscilla about the cancer diagnosis and pending surgery; Priscilla, in turn, could put out word to their network of Dartmouth friends. I knew I was overstepping my bounds; I also knew my sister's assumption that she could restrict news of her condition to family and a few select colleagues was unrealistic. Ann had attended Dartmouth; she worked as a fundraiser for Dartmouth; she lived on the outskirts of Dartmouth; she was having her surgery at the Dartmouth-Hitchcock Medical Center. "You're going to need your friends," I pressed. "All that love and support did Joe a lot of good." Firmly, Ann declined.

The next morning as my sister and I killed time in a small examining room, waiting for her to be rolled into the OR, Ann repeatedly thanked me for being there with her. Sensing an opening, I again asked if I could call Priscilla and maybe one or two of Jim's friends. This time, she relented and even told me which of Jim's friends I should contact. Five hours later, Ann was wheeled back out of the operating theater, an 11.5-inch incision, held together by forty-one staples, carved down the length of her chest. While she lay in the recovery area, Jim and I were ushered by her surgeon into a windowless consultation room.

He told us that one of the liver spots was too deep to inspect. And a lesion near the kidney was too "fixed" to be removed. He spoke of the chemo being palliative, not curative. He said maybe the [pending] chemo would shrink the remaining spots sufficiently to make them removable. "But," he reminded, "this is stage 4 cancer."

You'd never know it from the way Ann rebounded. Within hours of shaking off the anesthesia, she was not only ready to accept visitors; she was ready to entertain. When her boss dropped by that evening, their laughter echoed down the corridors. The next morning, a nurse rousted Ann from bed at 8:15, saying the day's goal was three short walks. By noon, my sister had put those three walks behind her. By evening, she'd upped the count to six. The following morning, she wandered so far that a nurse had to dial her cell phone to summon her back. After that, Ann didn't have time to stray so far afield. News of her condition had spread quickly, and friends, Dartmouth colleagues, and out-of-state former colleagues were beginning to arrive in groups large and small. Ann commandeered a lounge and there she would stay from morning to night, save for short jaunts, until she was released on day five, two days ahead of schedule.

During her first forty-eight hours home I continued to handle food shopping and errands, but it became increasingly clear to me that I was in the way. While Ann welcomed foot massages, she couldn't abide hovering. When I met Jim's comment that he felt a cold coming on with a suggestion that he sleep in another room, he said tersely, "I'm on top of it." Of course he was. What was I thinking? *After that it started to feel like every drawer I opened in the kitchen was impeding his movements.* I was reminded how difficult I'd found it to have a guest in the house during Joe's transplant, and only now realized how delicately Esme had navigated around me.

Before I headed back to New Jersey, Ann thanked me for putting out word to her friends and Jim's. Trying to hide such a huge secret, she acknowledged, was an unwanted burden. The outpouring of love and support had helped. Even so, Ann seemed less focused on prolonging life than on maximizing whatever time she had left. As she voiced her skepticism about chemo and returned again and again to her concerns about "quality of life," it was evident that Ann was seeing an endgame. I, like everyone in my family, encouraged her to give the chemo a chance.

But the truth? I hear my sister is dying. I called Lynn and she let me say it and wail . . . I keep thinking that Joe is my life, but Ann is my heart. This ache isn't the fear I felt with Joe. I can allow myself to consider the loss without risking getting lost myself. My life won't change shape if I lose Ann; but there will be a huge unfillable hole. I can't imagine the world without Ann. My love for her is without bounds.

Ann withstood eight aggressive rounds of chemotherapy over the next six months, the goal to make her a viable candidate for liver resection surgery. During this period, I seized on any pretext to call her. A development in the presidential race. A piece of Mom drama. A movie recommendation. I'm certain Ann knew exactly why I was calling.

Riding her wavelength was a challenge. Contrary to her description of herself and Jim as "take it as it comes" types, Ann questioned and second-guessed everything. Not entirely comfortable with her doctors and their proposed course of treatment, she developed a second network of doctors at the Dana-Farber Cancer Institute in Boston, whom she consulted after each new development. The two times she let me accompany her on her Boston rounds, it was painful to hear her ping-pong anxiously between her desire to transfer her care to Dana-Farber and her reluctance to saddle Jim with such a long commute. As I strove to reflect Ann's preferences and keep my own opinions out of the picture, I gained a deeper appreciation for my father's mirroring talents. And as I watched Jim, who really is a take-it-as-it-comes type, struggle to keep pace with Ann's jagged course, I realized how fortunate Joe and I were that we'd been able to settle quickly on our chemo and transplant teams, and not look back.

Harder still was Ann's habit of rushing to the hospital lab after each new set of scans to demand the results before her doctors had a chance to weigh in. Initially, her insistence on these sneak previews, which I think was Ann's attempt to feel in control of her treatment, stirred in me a combination of admiration for my sister and uneasy questions about myself. Why had I never thought to get my hands on Joe's labs? Should I have been more proactive? Had the two of us been lemmings? When it became apparent that lab write-ups are filled with scary-sounding jargon impenetrable to a layperson, my doubts subsided. Each time Ann leapt out ahead of her doctors, churning up days of anguished speculation, I caught a glimpse of the anxiety Joe and I had spared each other by sticking to Dr. B's day-at-a-time playbook. This neither convinced me our approach had been "right" nor diminished my admiration for Ann's proactive approach. But it did make me aware that it had been good luck, not a given, that Joe and I shared an inclination to "board the train and go for the ride."

For Ann's bumpier ride, I opened a back channel to a college friend, now a liver specialist in London. His e-mails gently and patiently untangled the medical jargon, and helped me put developments in perspective. When his message was encouraging, I shared it with Ann. When his words were qualified and careful, I waited with Ann to hear from her docs.

It's likely my brother Jonathan's lighter approach was more helpful to Ann than my earnest one. He dubbed her The Colon Kid and made good on the pledge he e-mailed her soon after her diagnosis: "Some phone calls, some brotherly pestering and no more than two colon jokes a week."

The best of us by far, though, was Joe. He had a gift for finding the humor in the absurdities and indignities of patient life. Ann credited Joe with teaching her how to handle cancer treatment, which, he'd warned, "Knocks you down so you can get back up so you can be knocked down again." She found inspiration in his continuing recovery. "I have a 1 in 3 chance of beating this," she wrote in an e-mail. "That's why I'm choosing to focus on Joe. He was much higher risk, and somehow he's managed to beat his leukemia. He's my hero."

In mid-March, Ann e-mailed a stunning update: "Great news! I'm now a member of the 6% Exclusive Club; that is, only 6% of stage 4 colon cancer patients fall into this category. In other words, I'm the 'miracle patient' du jour. The PET/CT scan showed no metabolically active metastatic disease in the lymph nodes or liver!

This is a very encouraging, cautiously optimistic sign." While the members of the Smolowe clan melted into a soggy mass of bawling relief, Joe fired back, "You know this really pisses me off! The very least you could have done was lose your hair! Life is unfair!"

I felt such joy that day.

It would be a long time before that feeling would come round again.

On March 28, 2009, eleven days after Ann's heartening news, Joe's sister phoned from Pasadena. "Short isn't doing well," Esme said.

"Should I come?" Joe asked.

There was no clear answer. We'd been through many medical emergencies with Joe's mother in recent years; she'd always rebounded. Then again, after much resistance, she'd finally checked into a residential hospice two days earlier. Joe wanted to make the trip. Almost a year had passed since his relapse; for months, he'd been commuting in and out of Manhattan, without incident, to help develop a new magazine. His transplant doctors acceded, provided Joe kept his nose and mouth covered with a surgical mask during the five-hour plane ride.

While Joe was mid-flight, Esme's husband phoned me. "It's over," he said.

Joe decided to remain in California for a few days to help Esme clean out Short's apartment. With him gone, I arranged for Becky's former sitter to stay at our house for a few days, then headed south for an overdue visit with my own mother. Through these many months of illness—Joe's relapse; Ann's surgery and chemo; Short's final decline—she, too, had been in poor health. But, her new eating-related dizziness aside, it was difficult to gauge whether Mom was any worse than she'd been for the last several years. She refused to discuss her symptoms and aches, which, according to my father, caused middle-of-the-night falls that left her writhing in pain on the floor. Each time we spoke by phone, Mom struck only one note: she was ready to go.

During my last visit, she'd said, "There's something I want to show you," and had gestured for me to follow her into the guestroom walk-in closet. Pointing to a shirt and slacks hanging in a plastic bag, she'd said, "That's what I want to be buried in." With both Joe and Ann battling so hard for life at the time, it had required an effort to keep my expression neutral as I said, "Okay." In my head, I was the Cher character in *Moonstruck*, smacking her upside the head and yelling, "Snap out of it!"

Now, I had a confusion of feelings as I touched down in North Carolina. Given that my mother-in-law had just died, I had little patience for my mother's relentless talk about her own readiness to go. On the other hand, Mom had been living with acute physical pain for a long time. Who was I or anyone else to say how much she should have to endure? I also arrived newly appreciative of my mother's consideration for the people she would be leaving behind. Where Short had left a chaos of unfiled papers, unsorted mail, and small savings accounts in banks scattered all over the country, Mom had her affairs meticulously in order: a living will, a burial plot, instructions for a memorial service, a list for the dispensation of her valuables. She even had a list of widows in her retirement village who she thought would make excellent dating material for my father. This underscored (somewhat comically, I thought) a message she'd been hammering at my father for years: "When I go, you should remarry."

She was so unsentimental about death, my mother. Life, as she saw it, was an eternal continuum not to be confused with the physical body; when the body gave out, the spirit exited, like a driver from a broken-down car, and continued on its journey.

Unlike Short, who'd clung to life, battling for every extra breath, my mother saw no reason to cling. To her, the final breath was a new beginning. She was interested in, even excited about, what came next. In her retirement community, she'd become the go-to person when families were wrestling with a loved one's final throes. Summoned to countless deathbeds, she'd whisper to a distraught son, daughter, or spouse, "Tell him it's okay to let go. Tell him you'll be fine." Calm and fearless about death, my mother, who counted Elisabeth Kübler-Ross among her close friends, had, like Kübler-Ross, helped so many people help their loved ones move on. She was, I heard again and again from people in her community, "a wonder."

Yes, she was. But she was also my mom. It was hard to swallow that she was both failing and failing to do anything much about it beyond entertain hospice workers a few times a week. On this visit, like so many before, I ground my teeth until my jaw ached as she repeated her final instructions for the zillionth time. By the time I packed to leave a few days later, I was, as usual, divided between my frustration at her focus on death and my uncertainty if I would ever see her again. "I love you," I said as I bent over her wheelchair to kiss her good-bye.

"Yes," she answered in a hoarse voice. "But do you like me?"

I bit the insides of my cheeks as I wheeled my suitcase to the car, threw it in the backseat, and slammed the door. I'd had enough. I just wanted to get in the car, hit the road, and—

Shit. We did this to each other, my mother and I. We tried so hard to be there for each other, and yet we almost always fell short. What if this really was the last time I'd see her? I retraced my steps, put my lips to her ear, and said, "Yes, Mom, I like you." Then I got out of there fast.

After I returned home, her question continued to nag. Which was more terrible, that she'd asked such a guilt-inducing question or that she'd felt the need to ask? Had she even meant it? Finally, I sat down at my computer and began a letter: "Dear Mom, You asked me if I *like* you. It made me realize how badly I've failed you as a daughter if I haven't communicated that in addition to (of course) loving you, there are many, many things I like about you as well. Here, belatedly and in roughly chronological order, are some of the reasons I *like* you—and like having you for my Mom."

I went on to offer eleven bulleted items that ranged from the ridiculous ("I really *like* you because you're the only Mom I know who tells dirty jokes") to the sublime ("I really *like* you because you've never told me how to raise my kid, but when I do ask for advice, you always offer something sensible and helpful"). The item that made me choke up because it felt the deepest and truest was the last: "I really *like* you because even though we almost never get it right, I know that you want to as much as I do—and so we keep trying. And therein, for me, is the heart of our friendship, as imperfect as it may be: I truly believe that we approach each other with goodwill each and every time; we try to do our best by the other each and every time; and when we fall short (each and every time), we don't give up. Instead, each of us resolves to do better next time—each and every time."

A few days later Mom phoned. "Thank you for that beautifully written letter. I will treasure it for as long as I live." I fastened on her second sentence and rolled my eyes. But when I heard from Dad and each of my siblings that she'd shown or read them the letter, I was glad I'd given her pleasure, and grateful she'd afforded me the opportunity to voice appreciation for things I'd taken too much for granted. What if she'd gone to her grave wondering whether I liked her? What if she'd died not knowing how deeply grateful I was for the many gifts she'd given me?

Whenever that day might be, I felt I had made my peace with my mother.

Joe, conversely, was having a hard time making peace with his. His time on the West Coast had expanded from an anticipated few days to a week as he and Esme laboriously made their way through haphazard mounds of papers, account statements, bills, and correspondences, much of it ancient trash can fodder. On his nightly phone calls home, I could hear his agitation building. Mostly he fumed about how long it was taking to clear out Short's modest one-bedroom apartment. She'd gotten rid of furniture, books, dog trophies, and dishware during a succession of moves from Wisconsin to Nevada to California. How could there still be so much stuff? Why was her estate in such chaos? Why was this taking so long? I clucked sympathetically, but I was amused. For as long as I'd known Joe, he'd been incapable of throwing away anything: reporters' notebooks, journalism clips, research materials, drafts of his plays, Playbills, receipts, even Stickies bearing illegible phone numbers. Our attic in Montclair was wall-to-wall Weasel boxes, a fire waiting to happen. I'd long since given up suggesting he cull the mounds.

It wasn't until Joe returned home that I realized a more serious issue underlay his agitation. His mother had been adamant that she didn't want a memorial service. Fourteen months earlier, Esme had orchestrated a remarkable gift for Short's ninety-fifth birthday: letters from friends, most of them, like Short, members of the dog fancy community that I, in turn, had compiled in a scrapbook. The rich trove of remembrances apparently had provided all the commemoration Short needed. Each time Joe or Esme pressed her to consider a memorial service, she snapped, "Who would come? All of my friends are dead." While her birthday scrapbook put the lie to that, her friends were scattered around the country. Short, I think, dreaded the possibility of an empty room.

Now Joe was having difficulty with her "no memorial" edict. While he wanted to honor her wishes, the lack of a commemorative event had left him with what he described as an uncomfortable feeling of suspension. As a result, he was having a much harder time dealing with his mother's death than he'd expected.

"Screw what Short wanted," I said, as capable of bluntness as my mother-in-law. "If you feel you need a gathering to achieve some sort of closure, then you should hold one. Wherever it is, I'll be there." Joe stared at me, unconvinced. "Wease," I persisted, "memorial services are for the living. You're the one who has to go on, not Short. Maybe Esme feels the same way. You should talk to her."

After a moment, Joe nodded. "Okay, I will."

I'm pretty sure Joe gave my suggestion thought over the next month. I'm pretty sure indecision about how he wanted to proceed caused him to delay phoning his sister. I'm also pretty sure Joe intended to have that conversation with Esme.

What I know for certain is that by stalling, Joe ran out his chance.

7

DEATH

MAY 4, 2009. *Joe has been complaining about numb feet for several months now. About 10 days ago (I think longer, but he dates it to there), he started slowing down, feeling a heaviness in his legs. Walking to his Manhattan office, he had to stop one day, completely depleted. Another day he walked up the Port Authority escalator and experienced the same effect when he hit the top. Ann is experiencing both—numbing and leg heaviness—while in chemo. But Joe's chemo is years behind him. He's also increasingly tired.*

In recent weeks, Joe's transplant team had packed him off to an assortment of specialists, who in turn ordered four MRIs, blood clot tests, a sonogram of his lungs, and a spinal tap. The neurologist suspected a recurrence of leukemia; the pulmonologist thought Joe's meds were the culprit. More tests followed. Meanwhile, despite Joe's windedness, congestion, sore throat, wracking cough, and thirteen-pound weight loss in three weeks, the transplant team saw no cause for alarm. Initially, I took their cue. My father was suddenly dealing with chest pains, my mother with continuing dizziness, my sister with chemo, my brothers with job losses. I didn't want to add needless worry to the list.

Joe didn't, either. Though he said he couldn't ever recall feeling so terrible, he continued to commute into the city, squeezing in work between doctor's appointments. At night, he resented my questions and offers of help, except when, too exhausted to do more than lie down, he required my attention. *Before, he needed me there and wanted me there. Now, he wants me there only when he needs me there, which he wants to believe is never. He accepts my assistance, as my mother does my father's, begrudgingly . . . What Joe needs most right now is for me to leave him alone. That, too, is caregiving: knowing when the person you are caring for does not want to take what you are offering.* A noble sentiment. But, like Joe, I was frustrated and irritable.

On May 8, Wease sounded so bad on the phone that I offered to accompany him to his latest diagnostic torture, a nerve test. When he didn't say no, I slipped away from *People* and together we rode the B train to the Upper West Side. As I watched him labor up the subway stairs, pause halfway down a short block to lean against a car, panting and exhausted, then collapse into a chair in the neurologist's waiting room, I finally got it: Joe was very sick. The neurologist thought so, too, and urged us to visit his transplant team—immediately.

Across town at Mount Sinai, the doctor on rotation that day listened to Joe's accumulating list of symptoms, then offered a new array of possibilities. Spinal tap side effects. Flu. A recurrence of GVHD in his lungs. *The sense I got from her was, Tough it out. The problem is I'm watching Joe's vitality drain more and more each day. He's not shaving, only occasionally bathing . . . He feels awful; he looks awful; his mood is cranky and angry.*

Over the next five days I felt like I was watching my husband disintegrate. No longer able to work, he sometimes sat immobile at the kitchen island, elbows propped on the counter, hands cupping his chin as he stared unblinking into space. Becky's former babysitter and I thought he eerily resembled his mother at the height of her decline. *Don't know what's going on. Don't know which symptom(s) is serious. Don't want to leave the house for fear I'm needed. Feeling trapped. Because Joe and I are pissy with each other right now, it's not gentle or loving . . . Makes it harder to "surrender" to shaping my days around him.*

Nighttime was no better. As we lay in bed, Joe's breath was now so shallow and labored that I found myself remembering Richard's description of his final night with his wife. A sudden shiver. An unfamiliar sound. Then, death. *Is Joe going to expire? Everything about him is unwell . . . I don't believe he's going to die, but I fear it. Short just died. My father just had a stent put in. Ann and her cancer. It's enough already; it's too fucking much . . . I'm scared. And if I'm scared, I can only multiply that many times over to arrive at Joe's mindset.*

Back when Joe was undergoing chemo, I'd soft-pedaled his condition in carefully crafted e-mails. Now, not wanting to believe we could be back in a place that required a revival of the Weasel Update, I instead fielded phone calls from family members, answering their questions with blunt descriptions of his frightening condition. *I don't know why I'm doing this. It isn't serving as a release valve. I get off the phone and don't feel a damn bit better. Maybe I'm doing it because Joe and I both feel his doctors aren't getting that something is terribly, terribly wrong. We want—we need—someone to hear us.*

On May 15, Joe called me at my office sounding so terrible that I persuaded him to take a cab into the city and meet me at Mount Sinai. When I entered the emergency room, I found him slumped in a chair, too dazed and exhausted to ask for help. Our return to Mount Sinai should have felt reassuring given the solid care Joe had received throughout his transplant and recovery. But this was different. No one in the ER knew Joe, so no one could appreciate how debilitated he'd become by his lengthening list of symptoms, which now included vomiting, diarrhea, fever, chills, laryngitis, and an inability to get or hold food down. The ER doctors saw a tall, somewhat gaunt guy with a raspy voice who looked more robust than most of their other patients. When a lung X-ray turned up nothing, they concluded the situation wasn't urgent. We were told that until Joe's doctors could free up a room in the transplant unit, Joe would remain in the ER. I reminded a succession of doctors that Joe's body was immune-compromised; none of them shared my concern that my husband was a target for every germ passing through the ER.

As the hours ticked by, I gave up on the doctors and began pleading with nurses to isolate Joe. Eventually that got him moved to a corridor at the rear of the ER. Though it was less trafficked, the thin curtain surrounding his bed provided no protection from neighboring patients' coughs and sneezes, let alone their small children, who ran up and down the dark hallway shrieking. Around the eighteenth hour, Joe's rasp now reduced to a whisper, I pulled out my cell phone, dialed his number, then handed my phone to a nurse. "*That's* what his voice usually sounds like," I said. As she listened to the deep timbre of Joe's voice mail message, a look of alarm crossed her face. Minutes later, Joe was rolled into a room with walls and a door. There, he would lie for the next twelve hours.

That thirty-hour horror show proved an apt curtain raiser for the drama about to unfold.

We'd always been so dutiful about getting on the train and going for the ride. Now it became clear that such a passage is possible only when the itinerary is clearly mapped. Initial treatment for leukemia is standardized; treatment for transplant complications is not. Over the next ten days, the many specialists who rotated through Joe's room couldn't agree what was ailing him, what tests to administer, which course of treatment to pursue. While they stood just outside his door, debating, sometimes bickering, with the transplant doctors about which aspect of his deteriorating condition should take precedence, Wease dropped another thirteen pounds, began to cough up hard chunks of unidentified matter, and lost his voice completely.

For the first time, I felt very alone. Despite my repeated pleas for a morphine dispenser, no one seemed to care that he was in pain. Despite Joe's rapid weight loss, days went by before anyone seconded my concern that he was getting no nutrition. No one could say if the damage to his lungs and vocal cords was permanent. Most disturbing, no one seemed to be in charge of Joe's case. Caught in a nightmarish version of the parable about the elephant and the blind men, with each specialist seeing a discrete part of Joe, I had the discomfiting sense I was the only person seeing the whole man—and the whole man was fading before my eyes.

Even after the dimensions of Joe's problems clarified, treatment remained elusive. To combat a severe recurrence of GVHD in his lungs, he needed to step up his intake of immunosuppressants; to tame newer lung invaders (fungal infection, parainfluenza, pneumonia), he needed to stop taking those meds. To work around a paralyzed vocal cord that was forcing food down his windpipe, he needed to be fed intravenously; the three attempts to insert an IV port yielded only blood clots.

It's hard to know if they're curing him or slowly killing him . . . This is the scariest thing we've been through, more even than the leukemia. There, we had dire thoughts for a few days, but death never felt close . . . Now, it feels looming.

On Day Three, Joe suddenly said, "Do you see that light?" Thinking he meant the fluorescent bulb behind his bed, I rose to turn it off. "Not that one," he said. "That one." Joe pointed to the left of his head. "Now it's over here." Slowly, his arm swept across his chest and he pointed to the right side of his head. "No, wait, it's right here. Bright." Closing his eyes, Joe drew his index finger to the middle of his forehead. "Can you see that?"

All sensation sucked up through my body and started buzzing in my head. "See what?"

With a tone of amazement, Joe described a mountain scene. Blue sky. Lush flowers. "I've never seen anything so beautiful. Wait! Now it's a beautiful beach with no one on it."

I could feel and hear the pounding in my temples. Shortly before dying, many people describe a tunnel of light. Others, my great-grandmother and mother-in-law among them, describe visits from dead loved ones. Those left to ponder such accounts tend to fall into one of two camps: they either regard the phenomena as evidence of an afterlife (that would be me) or they dismiss the episodes as hallucinatory bunk (that would be Joe). For my husband, the unwavering skeptic, to suddenly be describing a bright light, with a look of rapture on his face—

He was freaking me out. I grabbed Joe by both arms and yanked him to an upright position. "Do you see a tunnel of light?"

"No. It's bright. Like the sun."

"Don't follow that light," I said sternly.

Joe opened his eyes. When he seemed fully present, I said, "I thought you were dying. Do you want to go?"

"No," he said.

"Okay. Then if that happens again, tell whoever is there that you're not ready, that it's not your time."

When I entered his room the next morning—a visit that began with Joe telling me he'd dreamed of his own memorial service— Wease had an explanation for his unusual visions. Just prior to his hospitalization, he'd been working on a new magazine; one of his tasks had involved culling through photos of mountain vistas, beach scenes, and bucolic landscapes. The images he'd seen in his mind, he said, had been drawn from those stacks. True to his beliefs, Joe had separated the light and the images from any near-death context. I assumed that was that.

But Joe surprised me. "There are some things I want you to know, in case I die," he said.

Struggling to look receptive, I took my notebook from my purse. To him, it was a signal I was taking him seriously. For me, it was a necessity; I was too numb to hope I might accurately remember whatever he had to say.

Joe proceeded to tell me that he wanted Becky to have his Leica camera and copies of his novel and two full-length plays. He wanted his extensive collection of theater books to go to his cousin Bill, a fellow writer. The stuff he'd mailed from his mother's apartment a few months earlier that now sat in unopened boxes beneath his standing desk should go to his sister, along with a folder on his desktop containing his years of genealogical research. "Everything else, throw it away," he said. "I don't want you to feel saddled with my stuff the way I felt saddled with Short's."

"What about your journals?" I asked. "You want me to throw those away, too?"

"Yeah," he said, though not convincingly.

"Maybe I'll just put them in the attic and decide that one up the road," I said.

That seemed to sit well with him.

Next, Joe told me he wanted to be cremated, but had no preference where he would be buried. "That's really more about what the people left behind need," I said. I couldn't tell whether his answering shrug indicated agreement or indifference.

Joe continued that he regretted his mother hadn't had a memorial service. Reddening with modesty, he said he wanted one, but—

He paused, his blush deepening to a shade of embarrassment.

"What, Wease?" I coaxed.

"I just don't want the service overrun with Smolowes."

We both burst out laughing.

"I get it," I said, then ticked off the names of some of his closest friends. "People like that. People who really know you." With a smile, Joe indicated he liked the sound of that.

Several seconds of silence passed, then Joe said, "You're still young and attractive. You should remarry."

Though he spoke the words firmly, the expression on his face suggested hesitation. Was he uncertain that he meant it? Or was he uncertain that I was ready to hear it? "If I were lying where you are, I'd tell you exactly the same thing," I said. "We've had a happy marriage. Why wouldn't I want that for you again?" Joe's facial muscles relaxed.

Five minutes, ten minutes max. That's all Joe required to convey his dying wishes. He'd been calm, matter-of-fact, practical. Our laughter over the too-many-Smolowes thing had dissipated the numbing intensity of talking about his possible death.

Hours later as I stepped out of his room to head home, Joe called me back in. "Thank you," he said. "What you do is just incredible."

I was heart warmed—and chilled. This was more than our usual, just in case, "I love you." This felt like him telling me something he needed me to know before he dies.

The second weekend of Joe's hospital stay, we decided I'd bring Becky for a visit. Concerned that Joe's withered condition might upset her, I purchased matinee tickets to *Hair*, thinking this way the trip would end on an up note. Fortunately, Wease was having a better day and was out of bed, sitting in the reclining chair. When boredom began to set in, I suggested a stroll. It was slow-going, but Joe managed two laps around the unit. As we returned to his room I was riding the high of seeing him mobile—only to discover both Becky's purse and mine were missing. I opened every drawer, scoured every surface, got down on my stomach and checked beneath the bed, chair, and bureau. While Joe phoned the police, doctors and nurses rotated in and out the room, shaking their heads and clucking. A theft? In *this* unit? Unprecedented. Me? I felt as violated as if I'd been attacked in a house of worship. I wanted to take a shower.

But there was no time for that. Never mind that my wallet was gone, and with it my credit cards, money, and identification. Never mind that the *Hair* tickets were gone, and with them my hopes for a happy outing with Becky. Of more immediate consequence, my key ring was gone, and with it my key to our Subaru, parked outside the hospital. Leaving Joe to cancel my credit cards, I took a cab home, courtesy of the hospital, to fetch Joe's car key. Just when you thought it couldn't get worse, I thought, slumping miserably in the backseat. Within minutes, the driver, a chatty, sympathetic guy had me talking about other things. When I returned to Mount Sinai, I could hear Joe and Becky's laughter from a corridor away. That night, Wease would tell me by phone that they'd had a really good visit.

A few days later on a rainy afternoon, I drove to the closest DMV office, some twenty minutes from Montclair, to replace my driver's license. Knowing how finicky motor vehicle bureaucrats can be, I'd consulted the online DMV information to make sure I arrived armed with all the required pieces of identification. After standing in line for a half hour, I stepped up to the counter and set down my documents. The woman glanced at the papers and handed back my marriage license. "This is no good," she said. Yes, it is, I said. The DMV site says a marriage license counts as identification. "It's no good," she repeated. "We can't accept that as identification because you didn't change your last name." What the hell did that have to do with anything? "Don't get sassy with me. You need a different piece of identification. Next!"

I stormed out of the building into the rain, muttering to myself as I strode across the large parking lot. By the time I reached my car, I was drenched. "Godfuckingdamnit!" I screamed, kicking the car tires. "Godfuckingdamnit! Godfuckingdamnit!" I didn't care who saw me. "Godfuckingdamnit!" I didn't care who heard me. "Godfuckingdamnit!" I didn't care, period. "Godfucking—" I just . . . "God—" I just . . .

My amusement at the absurdity of it all began to drain my fury. My husband's leukemia. My sister's colon cancer. My mother's mystery ailment. My father's stent. My mother-in-law's death. Now, Joe's frightening relapse. Through two and a half years of worry and anguish, I'd held it together. In less than a minute, a DMV bureaucrat had reduced me to a ranting lunatic.

I got in the car. I drove home. I pulled out another document. I drove back to the DMV office. I got back in the line. Attila the Bureaucrat waved me forward. In minutes, I had a new license. "Thank you," I said.

"Next!"

At the end of week two, his condition still deteriorating, Joe said, "This is the beginning of old age"—a chilling statement coming from a guy long regarded as the Peter Pan of his college set. Until now, Wease had never expressed doubt that he would recover.

During these weeks, I was having trouble clearing time to spend full days with him. Becky, now a freshman member of her high school crew team, had weekday carpools to and from the Passaic River that required my presence in Montclair many afternoons; her regatta schedule took me to Philadelphia most

Sundays. Emotionally, Joe and I had gotten back on the same page the minute we met up in the ER, my resistance and his crankiness falling away. But I didn't feel a sense of relief when Joe was right in front me. It was unnerving to see him spend so much time in bed; it was anguishing to see him in so much pain. Because he could barely talk, each hour felt grindingly long. And I was having trouble masking my worry.

Death has been hanging so close . . . I am more resistant to going in to Mount Sinai . . . I think in part it's the not knowing. With the chemo and the transplant, we knew the trajectory, knew he'd go down, then come back up. Here it's never clear if the doctors have a handle on all the problems . . . It felt intimate with Joe the last time. This time, I just feel restless and impatient . . . Talking endlessly about his every pee, every poop, every cough is wearing. I don't know why it's so different this time. I can't do the 7–8 hour days. I do 3–4 mostly. I feel sad, scared, worn out. Becky is very huggy and sweet. That helps.

Unable to provide the diversion Joe deserved, I decided to tap some of the offers of "Anything." Each of the friends I contacted proved wonderfully responsive, supplying Joe with hours of distraction. But Mount Sinai, situated way over on the East Side, was a schlep for most of them. I couldn't bring myself to ask twice. So I leaned on his second cousin Caroline, who lived nearby. Prior to this hospital vigil, Caroline and Joe, who'd grown up in different parts of the country, had spent little time together. Now, as Caroline took it upon herself to pop in almost daily, they established one of those special, instant connections born of difficult circumstance. Within days, Joe and Caroline reached a place where they could say pretty much anything to each other. So did Caroline and I. It was such a relief to have another set of eyes on Joe, someone with whom I could compare notes about his labored progress.

One night a bronchoscope collapsed Joe's lung, precipitating a series of events so frightening to Wease that he phoned me near midnight. The next morning, he and I both fell asleep during my visit. *When I awoke, I said, "I sleep better when I'm near you." He said, "Me, too." He didn't want me to leave.* He then recounted a conversation he'd had with Caroline during which he'd talked about our marriage. She hadn't realized we'd been married so long, and expressed surprise at the length and quality of our union. Joe said he told her, "We've made it twenty-four years because of Jill. She gets all the credit."

Caroline responded, "Have you told her that?"

That evening, I concluded my journal entry, *He told me today.*

Then, Joe began to get better. At the end of the third week, I brought him home. A week later his transplant docs were so pleased by his progress that they said he could skip the following week's checkup. Finally, we could go to our country home in Pennsylvania, the only place Joe felt he could truly relax. That Friday after I got home from work, he, Becky, and I made the two-and-a-half-hour drive, with Joe at the wheel and in good spirits. The next morning, June 20, I awoke early, tiptoed out of the bedroom, and spent the next two hours in the rain weeding our shrubbery beds.

When I came back into the house around 10:00, Joe was up, looking and sounding good. While I showered, he drove to the local general store to buy his usual assortment of daily newspapers, then made himself breakfast. While he ate two fried eggs and toast, I stood on the opposite side of the kitchen counter, updating him about two friends who were dealing with cancer. A week earlier, I wouldn't have burdened Joe with such news. Now, with Wease on the mend, my friends' travails seemed sufficiently distant to tell him about an e-mail I'd received from one of them.

"The opening sentence was, 'My cancer is back.'" I cocked my head sideways. "In all the time you've been dealing with cancer I've never once heard you refer to leukemia that way. Do you ever think of it as 'my cancer?'"

"No," Joe said.

I grinned. "Me neither. I'm so proud of you that you've never let cancer define who you are."

Joe's head gave an aw-shucks wag. I laughed and touched his hand. "I should go dry my hair before it totally frizzes out."

Joe reached for a newspaper; I went into the first-floor bathroom. A few minutes later, thinking I heard a muffled noise, I snapped off my blow dryer. Nothing. I turned the dryer back on, then sufficiently puzzled, turned it off again and stepped into the kitchen.

He'd tilted back and was propped by the dining table. His arm was at such an odd angle that I thought maybe he was having a seizure. His color was odd. Yellow-tinted. The ABCs of a long-ago CPR course came rushing back to me: Air pipe, Breath, Compression. *I tilted his head more, pinched his nose, breathed into his mouth. I heard a gurgle, thought he was responding. Began pressing on his chest. I kept this up for several minutes. No response. I started screaming, "Joe! Wease! Come on!" Becky ran downstairs, said "Should I call 911?"* I looked across the counter at my fifteen-year-old daughter, momentarily awed by her composure. "Yes! I didn't even think of that," I said frantically. "Thank you. Do it!"

While Becky and I waited for help to arrive, I continued to blow air into Joe's mouth and apply inexpert compressions. It was during these ten, fifteen minutes that it began to sink in: Joe was dead.

Despite the frightening events of recent weeks, Joe's death felt unexpected and shocking. We had been through so much together during the last two and a half years: all that chemo, the stem cell transplant, the assorted post-transplant complications. After each setback, my completist husband had always tenaciously built back his strength. Wease, I sometimes joked, could take a licking, keep on ticking. Now, as I stood beside the local coroner watching five EMTs lower Joe to the floor, I had little confidence in my ability to do the same. While they draped a sheet over his body, time slowed to a crawl. *That's one minute without Joe*, I remember thinking. *That's two minutes without Joe . . .*

Somewhere in there I wrapped my arms around Becky. "You okay?" I whispered.

"I'm most worried about you," she answered. "It upsets me more to see you crying than to see Daddy that way."

That stopped the tears I hadn't realized were flowing. Suddenly, my mind was sharp, like the days right after Joe's diagnosis. I sent Becky upstairs to her bedroom, away from this horrifying sight. Then, I began to phone members of Joe's family and mine. My first calls were to Ann and Jonathan, who lived closest and, I knew, would drive to Montclair as soon as they could. Next, I called Esme. Then, I phoned Mount Sinai and got through to one of Joe's transplant doctors. "Joseph? Not Joseph!" she said, stunned. "I just saw him yesterday!" Several times I had to repeat my question, which in the moment felt urgently important: "Do you want to do an autopsy? If you think you can learn anything from his lungs that will help future transplant patients, Joe would want that."

Guided by the coroner, a gentle man whose face and name I don't remember, I then made more calls. I remember neither which person I phoned to get the name of a Montclair funeral home nor why I thought that particular person might offer good advice. I don't remember my conversation with the funeral home director, who I think also spoke with the coroner to arrange for the transport of Joe's body from Pennsylvania to New York. All of this required that I sign an autopsy form. Since there was no fax machine in the country house and the coroner needed to be certain that I received the form, I phoned my next-door neighbors in Montclair and asked to use their fax. I don't remember placing the call. They probably called me back after the form arrived, but I don't remember that either.

What I do remember about these phone calls is that to my own ear I sounded remarkably calm. I also remember that I never once said, "Joe is dead." Instead, I said, "Joe is gone." Each time, the person at the other end understood what I meant.

I have no sense how long all those calls took. How long the coroner and EMT crew remained in my kitchen. How long it took me to realize that I knew one of the EMTs, a woman Joe and I had often chatted with before lacing up our boots to cross-country ski on her property. When recognition finally dawned, she wrapped me in her arms and hugged me. That I remember.

Soon, an EMT, maybe her, took me gently by the arm. "We're going to move him now."

"Can I have a minute alone with him?" I asked.

After they stepped out of the kitchen, I knelt down and drew back the sheet. "I love you, Wease," I whispered, then bent and kissed Joe's face. As my lips touched his skin, the gesture felt false, melodramatic, even ghoulish. My sweet Weasel was gone.

Another minute without Joe. And another. I stood alone in the kitchen, dazed. The post-Joe world: everything familiar; everything changed. As my gaze took in the walls and the surfaces, my mind discreetly edited. Later I would recall the newspapers lying open on the counter, but not Joe's breakfast plate. I would remember the counter chair tipped backward against the dining table, but not who set it, empty, back in place. At some point a thought cut through my shock: I would not be returning anytime soon to this beloved getaway that for more than two decades had been Joe's and my private playground. With that, my focus on each passing minute gave way to a different thought, mantra-like, but not urgent: *Get home. Get home.*

Over the next hour, or maybe it was two, I slowly closed up the Pennsylvania house. With painstaking concentration, I emptied the dryer, folded the clothes and cleaned the lint screen. I washed, dried, and put away the dishes. I made sure the thermostats were set to fifty for when winter rolled in. Made sure the flue on the wood-burning stove was closed. Made sure every garbage can was emptied and every open carton in the fridge discarded. I bundled the trash in a large black plastic bag and deposited it in the driveway. Then, I went upstairs and wiped the bathroom counter, put stray laundry in the hamper, tidied the bedroom. I must have made the bed, but I have no recollection of looking at or touching the sheets and quilt that just hours earlier had covered Joe and me; that is another memory that my mind has edited out. After I turned off the fans and closed the upstairs windows, I returned to the ground floor to complete the final steps of the weekly closing-up ritual that Joe and I had always performed together to make sure we didn't forget anything. I closed and locked the windows; closed and locked the back door; closed and locked the garage door; turned off the water heater and water.

Though I didn't realize it as I carefully executed each of these tasks, I was receiving an important lesson about death. A master class. In my most fear-filled moments during Joe's illness, I'd entertained dark fantasies of what my life would be like without him. What I imagined was the boundless loneliness. What I dreaded was the sorrow, anhedonia, and depression that would rush in to fill the void opened by the absence of Joe's love and companionship. What I anticipated was the incredible heaviness of being as I waded through endless hours of an existence that I didn't want. In my conjurings, death was solely about the stoppage of Joe's life and the end of mine as I knew it.

Now, reality was quietly showing me that death is never only about death. It is also about the minute that follows death. And the one after that. And the one after that. Every detail of my imaginings had been colored by such enormity—the silence of a home not filled with Wease's deep, sonorous laugh; the holes in both Becky's life and mine; the aching pain of every minute—that there had been no room for the unremarkable aspects of daily life, the ones that take no note of death. Yet here I was, my husband's body barely out the door, dealing with laundry and dishes, garbage and thermostats.

Had I given any consideration to such mundane tasks, I would have predicted they could grow only smaller, disappear, in the face of such devastation. But in coming days, I would begin to realize I had it backwards. Rather than diminishing to inconsequence, the demands of everyday life offered something I could grab onto, something that could provide fleeting moments of distraction from my outsized emotions. These chores helped fill unwanted hours. They offered bite-size challenges I could undertake. Most importantly, they reminded me that though Joe's life had ended, mine had not. As I numbly went through the motions of closing the house, I registered only that last one: life goes on. It was, in its own way, very shocking.

At some point, Becky wandered back into the kitchen. As we talked, I felt chilly and, grabbing the closest thing at hand, pulled a zip-down sweatshirt over my tank top. Becky's reaction was immediate: "Oh, God, you're not going to be one of those people who wears black all the time, are you?" Not clear what she was talking about, I looked down. Black sweatshirt over black tank top. Widow's clothes. I shook my head and removed the sweatshirt.

I wouldn't remember that moment again until two years later when I read about it in my journal. But it must have made an impression. Except for Joe's burial, I would not dress all in black again.

On the trip back to New Jersey, I did something I rarely do: I drove at the posted speed limit. Though I felt lucid, I knew that my reflexes couldn't possibly be what they usually are. So, I stayed in the right lane and took it slow. During those three hours behind the wheel, I kept telling myself, *You cannot fall apart; you have to hold it together for Becky.* I don't remember what Becky and I talked about, beyond my asking her to phone Esme to let her know we were headed home. A journal entry reminds that Becky told me she'd already informed her friend Helena, via video chat, about Joe's death; also, that Helena's mother phoned and spoke with Becky.

When we came through the kitchen door in Montclair, my first thought was, *Why was I in such a rush to get home? Joe isn't here.*

Minutes later, the front doorbell rang. It was Helena and her mother, a pasta dinner in hand. Neighbors from down the street quickly followed. Soon, the phone began ringing with calls from friends, both in and out of town. How word had traveled so quickly, I have no idea. My next-door neighbors turned up at the kitchen door with bagels, lox, cream cheese, and a printout of the autopsy form. Another neighbor arrived toting twelve-packs of soda. Then, to my great relief, Ann, followed by Jonathan, pulled into the driveway. My formal period of mourning had begun.

Collapse of some sort, I assumed, was inevitable.

8

PRECONCEPTIONS

IN FACT, WHAT FOLLOWED BORE LITTLE RESEMBLANCE to what I thought I knew about grief. Yes, I experienced moments when I felt choked by sorrow, hollowed by loneliness, overwhelmed by Joe's absence. But they were—and three years on, still are—just that: moments. To my surprise, my feelings of devastation were intermittent, not all-consuming; disorienting, not unhinging. Grief, for me, was neither the unremitting quagmire of despair I'd experienced twice with depression, nor the total shattering I'd encountered in memoirs, novels, and films.

Magical thinking? I encountered it just once. Two, maybe three days after Joe died, I was sitting in the kitchen drinking coffee when the movement of a tall male figure caught my eye. *Wease!* I thought, the word forming on my lips to greet my husband, as I had every morning of our married life. When the person rounded corner, it was Jonathan, not Joe.

As for Kübler-Ross's grief cycle, I have found no resonance over the last three years in any of its five stages. Denial? From the moment I bent down to kiss Joe good-bye, I understood that the body in front of me was a corpse. Joe was gone. Anger? The closest I came was something I wrote the day after Joe died. *Today Joe is gone one day. Today [Joe's father] Al is gone four years. Al was 96 going on 97. Joe was 66 going on 67. I want those thirty years.* Bargaining? My already-weak inclination to pray (*Please, please, please*) withered entirely after Joe died. Depression? Given my prior history, I began a preemptive course of Paxil the night of Joe's death. Four months later, no longer concerned that a miasma of depression might smother my grief, I put the pills back in the cabinet. Acceptance? If that means I understand Joe is never coming back, I was clear on that point from the moment the EMTs covered his body with a sheet. If it means I no longer awake mornings thinking about Joe, then I am now there. If it means I've rebuilt a life in which my relationship with Joe is no longer the central organizing principle, then, yes, I've done that. But if acceptance means I find it acceptable that Joe is gone, then, no, I have not achieved acceptance, and I'm hard-pressed to believe I ever will.

The preconception that held on most tenaciously was my assumption that at some point I would "collapse." I didn't picture myself curled on the floor in an inert heap. Rather, what I anticipated was a gradual ebbing of will until there came a day when my sorrow trumped my inclination to keep going. Like the title character of Herman Melville's *Bartleby the Scrivener*, I would sit down and, overtaken by a feeling of "I would prefer not to," I wouldn't get back up for some undefined period of time. This matched the mental image I carry of my paternal grandmother, who for more than a decade after my grandfather's death spent hours each day in her reading chair, a thick novel open on her lap, staring into space. It matched the image of Lynn's grandmother, who for decades spent her days lying on her living room couch, one arm draped over her eyes. It matched the images I remembered from movies and memoirs of bereaved people so consumed by pain that they could do little more than wander through the empty rooms of their homes, their minds fogged by memories.

Within days of Joe's death, an artist friend sent me a parable she'd written about grief. On the cover was a black-and-white photo of a person prone on a bed with a sheet pulled over his/her head. For me, that picture epitomized my sense of grief. The withdrawal. The isolation. An opaque world stripped of air and light. The image took root in my mind and was soon embroidered with details, none of which drew from any previous experience I'd had with heartache or pain, yet seemed very real.

I keep waiting for the moment of collapse, perhaps because I can picture it so clearly: me curled on my side in bed, sheet pulled over my head, my body alternately trembling and heaving. I know the soundtrack, too, a mix of gut-wrenching sobs, feathery gasps and fingertips clawing the pillow beside me, the one that served as a landing pad for Joe's head . . . There I will lie, unable to eat or sleep, think or not think. Oblivious to the accumulating hours and mounds of Kleenex, I will simply surrender to memory. The recaptured moments will be happy ones, designed to hollow my brain, body and soul as I inventory all that I have lost. At some point, maybe, one of my concerned siblings or friends will tiptoe in with a tray of tomato soup (Joe's favorite) and toast, and whisper, "Try to eat something."

To my surprise—to my relief—that day never arrived.

Instead, though Joe was rarely more than a few minutes from my thoughts, I functioned much as I normally do, albeit with an oscillation of emotions more intense than usual. I had my ups; I had my downs. I laughed at times; I cried at times. I talked (though not as much as usual). I listened (with greater care than usual, since my thinking was fuzzy at times). I shopped for groceries (with less focus than usual). I tended to my daughter (with greater vigilance than usual). I had moments when the rush of sorrow felt like a tidal wave taking me under. But then I resurfaced and carried on.

It would be absurd to suggest that friends, relatives, and colleagues filled the vacuum opened by Joe's absence. That was a void nobody could fill, nor did I expect anyone to. Like most loving marriages of longstanding, Joe's and mine had been a unique fabric woven from threads meaningful to only the two of us. Our sturdy tangle of obligations and expectations, conflicting agendas and hard-won compromises, mutual goals and reassurances, individual disappointments and shared joys had been shot through with that golden thread that often keeps a marriage intact when the fabric threatens to fray: unwavering exclusivity.

The luxurious expectation of "just the two us" now gone, my daily habits no longer worked for me. Normally, I spend chunks of solitary time each day reading, writing, and thinking; if I don't spend enough time inside my head, my mood can turn cranky. Though that had changed when Joe got sick and I spent as much time with him as possible, I still used the late-evening hours to sink onto the living room couch in front of a mindless movie and let my thoughts sift through the day. Now, I preferred not to be alone with my thoughts.

The first two weeks I didn't need to seek out companionship. People simply came, day and night, a flow of traffic that I dubbed my "free-range shiva." They brought words of solace and moments of distraction, tight hugs and daunting amounts of food. After years of resisting people's attention and concern during Joe's illness, I now welcomed the company and the commiseration, gaining an appreciation for what Richard had meant when he'd told me, "I find the cards, the calls, people staying in touch tremendously comforting."

I also experienced a peculiar physical lightening that made me feel younger. Days passed before I put my finger on it: the weight of worry had lifted. Only after it was gone did I realize how heavily Joe's shaky health had been weighing on me—literally.

That I could feel anything other than sorrow was an unexpected gift. Whenever a positive emotion broke through—amusement;

comfort; affection; gratitude; relief—I latched onto it. Around day four, the widowed colleague from whom I'd recoiled shortly after Joe's diagnosis emerged from her car bearing a plate of brownies and radiating happiness. "Wow," I said. "You look fantastic." Cocking her head shyly, she said, "I have a new boyfriend." I don't think anyone could have delivered a more heartening message. For a moment, I felt happiness and hope—two emotions I was surprised I could access, however briefly, so soon after losing Joe.

During these weeks, either Ann or Jonathan was also on hand each day and night to ensure that Becky and I were never alone. Ann, who was the more frequent guest, handled the visitors and phone calls I was too drained to take; relayed information to my anxious parents in North Carolina; took Becky shopping to prepare for camp. Buoyed by her energy and surrounded by my friends' commiseration and goodwill, I was reminded how rich my life was. In case I was failing to register this safety net of support, Ann called it to my attention several times.

Late one morning before guests began to arrive, she put her arm around my shoulder and asked, "How are you doing, Meus?"

"I'm doing better than I might have anticipated," I said.

With that, Ann abandoned her concerned tone and launched into a series of short, declarative sentences that highlighted why I would pull through. Mirroring strengths and reframing weaknesses she knew I perceived in myself, she said, "You have good self-esteem. You have a passion for writing. You're fifty-three, with a young daughter. You have a rich circle of friends who are being supportive. You and Joe expressed your love and covered what needed to be covered; you have no regrets. You *are* social, more than you give yourself credit. You're holding court even at your worst."

Much as I appreciated others' caring acknowledgments of my grief, I *needed* reinforcement of my tentative sense that I could hold up. I got out my reporter's notebook and asked Ann to repeat her list. I wanted something to consult when I was feeling overwhelmed by sadness, loneliness, or doubts about my future.

As one day bled into the next, I began to realize that my most dreaded preconception might be misplaced. *Now into the third week. I'm more clear-headed than I would have anticipated . . . I can think and do things . . . My free-range shiva helped a lot. Made me realize that I have a life in Montclair, one that stands even with Joe gone . . . People have been amazing. Writer friends. Pennsylvania friends. New York friends. Neighbors. I didn't want to be "that woman" when Joe was sick. Now I am a different, more appalling kind of "that woman," but there's no hiding it. Don't even try. I take energy from encounters, especially from people who are high energy. They lift my spirit . . . I had thought when I saw the abyss after Joe's diagnosis that I would have to "reimagine" my whole life. I no longer think that's true.*

I don't mean to suggest that I ran away from my pain and loneliness. Even if I'd tried, constant collision with Joe's absence—the empty chair and lack of running commentary about newspaper stories at breakfast; the lack of humorous e-mails throughout the day; the silence that replaced Joe's dinner conversation, his booming laugh, his noisy cookie crunching as we watched TV; the vacant half of the bed at night—made avoidance impossible. But it didn't take long for me to realize that what I was feeling this minute might not be what I would be feeling the next. When my yearning for Joe rushed at me with sometimes-breathtaking force, I tried to practice what Joe and I had learned during his hospitalizations: stay in the present and don't get ahead of yourself. One minute at a time. One hour. One day.

Back in my midtwenties, when I was struggling with the first of my two episodes of clinical depression, I had a therapist who tried to convince me not to fight my pain so hard. "Just sit with it," she used to instruct.

"How?" I would answer, as I twisted myself into ever-deepening despair.

Now, for the first time in my life, I was able to sit with my pain. My loss of Joe. My loss of Joe and me. My daughter's loss of her father. Our loss of the three of us, what we called our Becky sandwich. My loss of the life that I assumed I would be living for several decades to come. Unlike most of the anguish that had blown through my life, bringing with it a tailwind of complicating questions (Did I bring this on myself? Can I handle this better? Am I overreacting?), this sorrow required no self-justification, explanation, or apology. To me, the pain seemed not only appropriate and understandable; it seemed necessary.

Soon, my most intense moments of grief settled into a pattern. Once a day, usually around dusk—the time of day when Joe and I used to reconnect after our separate workdays—I would feel a huge wave of sorrow rising up in me. If people were around, I pushed it down. I had no desire to share these overpowering waves of grief. This was for and about Joe; for and about me; for and about us. Where the pain came from, what the feelings of loss involved, were too personal, too special, too impossible to explain. But if I was alone, I surrendered without resistance, letting my grief take full hold and toss me where it might. I sobbed, keened, pounded the floor with my fists, choked on the mucus clogging my nose and throat, emptied boxes of Kleenex, and whispered over and over, "Where are you, Wease? Where are you?" These crying jags, which went on for many months, rarely lasted more than twenty minutes. By the fourth month, I trusted that I could tolerate them.

I disappear through a hole at the center of the earth. Then I

resurface and go on. I've come to understand that I will resurface,
that as much as those moments hurt, I know I will push back up and
be okay.

Even the most unpleasant aspects of the post-death rituals proved
less upsetting than I might have anticipated, had I thought about
them (which I hadn't). Joe had lifted the burden of one decision by
telling me that he wanted to be cremated. That left the selection of
a cemetery, a plot, and an urn. My sister attended me every step
of the way, at each step reminding, "It was such a gift that Joe told
you what he wanted. You don't know how lucky you are." Through
the years, Ann had lost close friends, some of those losses involv-
ing sudden deaths where there had been no opportunity to discuss
dying wishes. She'd seen grief-stunned families anguish as they
tried to divine what their departed loved one would have wanted.

Me, I knew what Joe wanted. That spared me any of the debate,
hesitation, equivocation, frustration, or anger I'd seen dramatized
on the five seasons of *Six Feet Under*. My meeting with a local
funeral home director lasted less than a half hour. Minutes before
the appointed time, Ann and I ducked out of the free-range shiva,
an informal affair that reflected Joe's and my casual lifestyle. I'd
been dressing in accordance with the warm weather—shorts, tank
tops, flip-flops—and, per Becky's edict, no black. Despite my *Six
Feet Under* bona fides, it didn't occur to me that a funeral home
visit might require more formal attire.

I rang the front bell and after a minute the door creaked open to
reveal an overly tall man with an overly somber expression on his
face. When he looked at Ann and me in our fun-in-the-sun clothes,
clearly uncertain which one of us was the grieving widow, it stiffened my resistance to a maudlin encounter. "Lurch," I whispered to

Ann. Suddenly, we were in Addams Family territory, the absurdity of him, of us, of the moment leaving us biting our bottom lips in order to not burst out laughing. Escorting us to a darkened room, Lurch posed a series of questions that I don't recall, then stood and said he would now show me the casket room. I shook my head. "My husband will be cremated," I said. "I need an urn." Our visit to the urn room lasted less than a minute. My eyes scanned the shelves and when I spotted a simple silver urn in keeping with Joe's taste, I said, "That one." As I turned to leave, Lurch said, "Don't you want to see—"

"No," I said.

Lurch then tried to engage me in chitchat about the funeral and the services he could provide. "No need," I said. "The burial will be a family-only affair with no religious officiant." When Lurch tried to take my hand, I declined by flattening my fingers against my thigh. I didn't know this man; I didn't want his consolation. Lurch was brilliant, however, on the logistical arrangements. He'd already gotten Joe's remains to Manhattan for an autopsy; now he told me he would make sure the cremated ashes got back to Montclair and on to the cemetery in time for the funeral once I set a date.

Back outside, Ann and I waited just long enough for Lurch to close the heavy front door before we dashed into the parking lot and doubled over, laughing hysterically. It felt good, that laughter. Inappropriate as I knew it was, it displaced some of my upset about the all too obvious: I'd just chosen the urn in which I was going to put my husband's ashes in the ground.

Our next task: selection of a burial site. Joe had left the choice up to me, and thankfully Becky had a preference that provided guidance. "I want to be able to visit Daddy," she said. That made me think of a local cemetery tucked behind the cooperative preschool Becky had attended as a tot. I now learned that it was actually two cemeteries, one religious, the other nondenominational. The proprietor of the second guided Ann and me to a small field where the plots were small, appropriate for an urn, and the tombstones were flat to the ground. When I reported back to Becky, she said, "But how will the flowers stand up when I bring them?"

Ann and I did a second reconnaissance. When I explained the headstone situation to the cemetery director, he said, "Monument." Monument? I echoed. "It's not a headstone, it's a monument," he said pompously. Fine, monument, whatever, I need one that stands up. "It's important to use the proper language," he persisted. I cocked an eyebrow at Ann. Was this guy for real? "What a jerk," Ann muttered and with a nod signaled, *Let it go.* I was so grateful she was there to witness and commiserate.

This time we were shown to an area abutting a heavily trafficked road. "Too noisy," I said, thinking of Becky's future visits. I turned, and that's when I saw it: the playground where Becky used to romp with her friends. Joe had been an active co-op dad. Maybe while visiting this sad spot, Becky would also remember happier days on the playground with Daddy. I walked toward the quieter center of the cemetery, keeping my eye on the playground. "Is there anything in this area?" I said, once I'd reached a point where the noise was less noticeable. After some tussling, I got what I wanted: two spots beneath a shady tree with an unobstructed view of the playground. I plan to be cremated, too; Joe and I would both fit.

On the drive home, Ann and I replayed the exchange with the cemetery director. "No, no, it's a monument, Meus," Ann lectured with mock consternation.

"But I'm just a poor, grieving widow," I said, turning on the melodrama. "Is it really so important what the fuck I call it?"

"You need to get it right," Ann said sternly.

Again, laughter helped.

That was it for burial arrangements. Having my sister by my side steadied and strengthened me—though I have no idea how

Ann navigated these tasks with such humor and grace. Somewhere along that short circuit, I vaguely realized she was making mental notes of things that needed to be done. For her.

A few weeks later, Esme accompanied me on the final task: selecting a, um, monument. While we walked around the cemetery hunting for a stone that we thought Joe would have liked, I told my sister-in-law about the absurd exchange I'd had with the cemetery director. We then proceeded to a stone yard, where I told the guy behind the counter that I wanted to order a headstone. "A monument," Esme slyly corrected.

And that was that. Once my choices were made, I did not think about them again.

My eleventh day of mourning, I had an appointment with Joe's and my attorney, Grace, to begin the process of settling Joe's estate. Though heartened by how well I was holding up, I knew my brain wasn't operating on all cylinders. So I asked Lynn, my backup brain, to accompany me to Grace's office.

The notes that I took during this meeting detail the items we covered: rolling over Joe's various bank accounts; dealing with Social Security, death taxes, term insurance, real estate tax returns, my deceased mother-in-law's estate; changing my beneficiary forms; changing the deeds on the car and two houses; procuring letters of testamentary and death certificates. In time I would come to think of these various tasks as the Dance of Death. Bite-sized and doable, each bureaucratic detail typically required multiple phone calls, letters, and e-mails to achieve resolution. Because each matter progressed in stages, often months apart, I had to pay close attention to what was said during any given phone conversation and take meticulous notes. I was glad for these small distractions.

As I checked the items off my to-do list, it heartened me to see that I remained a functioning human being.

What I remember most clearly about my meeting with Grace, however, has nothing to do with any of those details. I've known and admired Grace, a calm and forthright woman, since 1994, when she walked Joe and me through the closing on our Montclair house. Our encounters since then had always been in a professional context, but given the issues—wills, living wills, mortgage refinancing, estate planning, guardianship of Becky—our conversations often had touched on the personal. At some point, Grace had shared the painful news that her twentysomething daughter had Lou Gehrig's disease, to my mind the cruelest way to go. A year earlier, her daughter had passed away.

Perhaps because I knew that Grace had experience with grief, I responded to her "How are you doing?" with candor. "Better than I would have expected," I said. "I'm still waiting for the moment when I fall apart."

A look of surprise flickered across Grace's features. "You won't," she said, her tone matter-of-fact. "You're strong, like I am. I didn't collapse after my daughter died. I'm just not that kind of person— nor are you. You'll cope just fine."

"I recently talked to two widowed people, one a man, one a woman," I said. "They both told me exactly the same thing: it takes five years to get over grief."

"Oh, no. It won't take you that long," Grace said. "That doesn't mean you won't go on missing Joe. I miss my daughter every day. But I also have a lot going on in my life. You do, too." She talked about my daughter, my job, my book projects, my friends. She spoke about my strength, my competence, my ability to cope. She applauded my decision to return to work the following week; she, too, had returned to work soon after her daughter's death.

I hung on Grace's every word. Here was someone a year ahead

of me in what I still thought of as "the grief cycle," offering me an alternative to paralyzing sorrow. In her scenario, I would keep putting one foot in front of the other, just as I've always done. In her scenario, I would be, as she was, profoundly sad, but I would keep going because I had a life worth living.

"That was amazing," Lynn murmured during the drive home. "Grace is so wise."

When I asked what had struck her as amazing, Lynn spoke about Grace's "obvious pain, yet utter calm."

Usually when Lynn and I speak intimately, I am aware of her sensitivity and perceptiveness. Now, as I listened, I was struck instead by how differently we'd heard Grace. While I, too, had found the conversation "amazing," it wasn't Grace's blend of pain and calm that had made an impression. Rather, it was her assumption that I, like she, was coping well. That had been clear from her opening "How are you doing?" which she'd posed in the same down-to-earth tone she always employed. Her inflection had borne no trace of God-how-awful sympathy; no you-need-a-hug effusion; no you-must-be-a-total-basket-case concern. Instead, unlike anyone else, Grace had addressed me in a tone that conveyed her assumption I was still the steady Jill she knew. That, in turn, had led to a conversation focused on coping, rather than commiseration.

Lynn also expressed amazement about Grace's "generosity and candor." While I greatly appreciated Grace's openness, it hadn't struck me as surprising. My shiva visitors had included a widow and a widower, neither of whom I knew particularly well. Yet both had been responsive to my questions about their changed lives. Their willingness to talk so intimately had reminded me of Richard's generous candor after Joe's diagnosis.

Just as my conversation with Richard had left a deep impression, so did my talk with Grace. Her demeanor, words, and tone all suggested that she'd absorbed her heartbreaking loss without coming unglued. I took from our conversation something I hadn't realized I needed: "permission" to be all right.

That may sound odd, but the tide of sympathy that engulfs the newly bereaved is almost uniformly colored by the assumption that a grief-stricken person is, for a time, completely lost to sorrow. I knew I wasn't lost. Twice, I'd experienced just such a total loss of self while in the throes of depression. Trapped in a mental solitary confinement that allowed no room for thoughts of anything but my misery and inability to escape it, my emotional range had become static, my thoughts tiresome and repetitive, my comprehension dulled almost to the point of dysfunction. I took no pleasure in any place, any activity, any interaction. Being with other people was painful and required effort; being with myself was even more painful and required the most effort of all. The anhedonia of depression had been intolerable.

The sorrow of grief, I was discovering, was not. Much of the time it still allowed me to register and be a part of the world around me. I could tune in and out of conversations; concentrate on small tasks; even be distracted from my pain long enough to experience other emotions, albeit within a much-diminished range. A few months after Joe's death, I told a friend who, like me, had endured two depressions, "I lost Joe, but I haven't lost myself."

"I understand exactly what you mean," she said.

That relativity gave me perspective on my pain. No matter how bad my days got, I knew they could be worse—which made me wary that the worst was yet to come. It also produced intermittent feelings of guilt. Surrounded by concern and sympathy, the pressure to follow the more familiar script was so strong that I even had a few moments when I asked myself the truly unthinkable: had I not loved Joe as much as I thought?

Maybe I'm cruising for a plunge . . . All in all, I'm doing okay. Which surprises me. And relieves me. And makes me feel a little guilty. Is it because I was exhausted by the caretaking that I feel younger? . . . Am I okay because I know I did my very best for Wease? I hope so.

As the four-month anniversary of Joe's death neared, I thought of myself as "okay." I was becoming more recognizable to myself. In early August I'd written, *I think I'm nearing the end of wanting people around me constantly. It's exhausting.* My tolerance for being That Woman was wearing thin. Joe's absence and my sadness were with me all the time; I didn't need constant reminders from other people. I was a single parent now; I couldn't afford to be Morose Mommy. Additionally, my own mother was fading. My sister's colon cancer was metastasizing. At *People*, we were adjusting to a newly reduced staff. If I had a cloud of grief hovering over me all the time, I couldn't be the mother, daughter, sister, and colleague I wanted to be. Even so, I was having trouble accepting that it was okay to be okay. After almost three decades with Joe, shouldn't I be more of a wreck? Wasn't my "okayness" disrespectful of our love and his memory?

Late that October I spoke by phone with a friend in the advanced stages of uterine cancer. Our conversation was animated, as were her days as she plowed ahead writing a book that she was determined to finish. Her buoyancy prompted me to tell her about my own unexpected steadiness. She asked if I was familiar with the bereavement work of clinical psychologist George Bonanno, and pointed me toward his new book, *The Other Side of Sadness*.

There is a Buddhist proverb popular in yoga circles: "When the student is ready, the teacher will appear." I was a ready student; Bonanno would prove my teacher. His decades of research offered a picture of grief vastly different from Kübler-Ross's familiar portrait. According to Bonanno, my okayness, what he called "resilience," was no anomaly. Rather, it was the norm for better than half of the bereaved population. In sentence after sentence, Bonanno described my own perceptions and experience:

"We imagine grief to be a relentless shadow . . . overwhelming and unremitting." So, my expectation that grief would be an unyielding chokehold was typical.

"The good news is that for most of us, grief is not overwhelming or unending. As frightening as the pain of loss can be, most of us are resilient. Some of us cope so effectively, in fact, we hardly seem to miss a beat in our day-to-day lives." Wait, so it was neither unusual nor unseemly to return to work two weeks after Joe's death?

"It is easy to become suspicious when a bereaved person seems too happy or at ease. 'Is this some sort of denial?' we might wonder. Or worse, maybe the person never really cared about the loved one in the first place? . . . After many years of studying bereavement, I've found no evidence to support any of these ideas." Oh, thank God.

Or rather, thank you, George Bonanno. After reading his book, I stopped wondering and worrying whether it was okay to be okay. Grappling with sorrow and loneliness was hard enough. I was relieved to be done with the additional burden of feeling guilty that I was coping as well as I was.

9
GRATITUDE

WHILE PERSPECTIVE HELPED, it didn't spare me devastating moments, each day, every day. The ones that blindsided tended to hit hardest. The first time I confronted a medical form offering only three choices—single, divorced, or married—I welled up. *I am none of the above.* When I got to the part requiring two "in case of emergency" contacts, the tears cascaded as I wrote in the names of my younger brother and a neighbor. *All I could think was: How many people does it take to fill Wease's shoes. Not nearly enough.* Parents' night at Becky's high school wrung me out. *All those couples in the auditorium whispering to each other. Where was Wease to whisper, "This principal is so boring!"?* So did the prospect of phoning the bank holding the mortgage on our house; thanks to Joe's life insurance policy, I was now able to pay off the balance on our fifteen-year loan. *This should be us, burning the damn mortgage. Popping champagne. Paying off a mortgage; what an accomplishment. It just hurts.*

For a time, I experienced the world through a foggy lens. I'd wonder why I hadn't heard from so-and-so, only to be reminded that so-and-so had called or dropped by an hour earlier. Far clearer was my inner world. There, Joe was a constant and vivid presence. I saw him towel-draped in the bathroom, flossing his teeth. Nude on the bedroom carpet, his appendix scar prominent as he did his morning sit-ups. In the living room, performing his wacky bow-wow dance. On Becky's bed, reading *A Mother For Choco* aloud for the zillionth time. In the kitchen, brushing our dog's teeth. In a *People* hallway, winking at me over the heads of colleagues. In the UN chapel, beaming up the aisle as I approached to exchange marital vows.

Photos of Joe were so overpowering that I had to avert my gaze from the wall of framed five-by-sevens on our second-floor landing that documented our life together. Had I lived alone, I might have taken some of them down, but there was Becky to consider. That concern didn't extend to the master bedroom, where the sight of Joe's possessions was so distressing that I quickly cleaned out his closet and drawers, saving little more than his watch, wallet, Yankees baseball cap, and T-shirts (which I slept in every night for the next year). Family videos, once a source of laughter and pleasure, accumulated dust. Even the thought of viewing them chilled me.

Again and again, bereavement converted a cherished memory or object into a source of pain. Each time, the sting was fresh. Yet, the pain never surprised. Months into Joe's treatment, I'd written, *There isn't any real way to prepare yourself for someone's absence. I am aware that when I fantasize darkly about him dying, that I have a safety net: He is here.* Now, Joe was gone. No safety net. I expected extreme pain.

What I didn't expect was that the feelings of extreme pain would be attended by feelings of extreme gratitude. Even stronger than the appreciation I'd experienced during Joe's illness, this torrent of thankfulness registered people's kindness with a hyperalertness. Deeply, intensely, I felt appreciation for what remained good in my life. My wonderful daughter. My concerned parents. My supportive siblings. My attentive friends. My accommodating colleagues. My considerate neighbors. I was also keenly aware of the many variables that were sparing me a greater sense of dislocation. I had a job that provided steady income and work I enjoyed. A lovely home that, not insignificantly, I felt competent to administer solo. A community that surrounded Becky and me with support. Rather than having an impulse to flee a town filled with memories of Wease, I wanted to stay put. I had a life in Montclair, rich with friendships that were independent of and unhaunted by memories of Joe. Despite my desolation, I was aware that I was very fortunate. While Joe's death had hollowed out the center of my life, the infrastructure remained sturdy.

All of this, I began to see, was helping me to cope with Joe's absence and to recognize that though life without him was undesirable, it *was* imaginable. Was this my survival instinct kicking in? A genetically encoded balm? Whatever it was, my Oprah moment had arrived.

What propped me up most during those first months was the realization that I had no lingering regrets about the time Joe and I had spent together. Through the decades, we had drifted toward, not away, from each other. We'd remained each other's best friend, most reliable critic and sounding board, most trusted confidante. Joe's health crisis had drawn us still closer. During his hospitalizations, when we'd spent so much time alone together, we'd said what needed to be said. There were no outstanding issues between us, no unresolved disagreements, no words of affection left unspoken.

Neither illness nor death had served as a wakeup call to remind me why I loved Joe. Despite our years of close proximity, I'd remained alert to his interesting turn of mind and conversation, his humor and determination, his loyalty to family and friends, his trustworthiness and strong ethics, his boyish delight in new situations, people, and places. Sure, we'd had our rounds, particularly over starting a family. But after Becky entered our lives in 1995, Joe threw himself into parenting with such unbridled love, energy, and imagination that it was a rare day I didn't pause to watch the two of them and think, *This is amazing.*

Still, the years had brought their share of compromises and adaptations that had long since settled into expectations and assumptions. Much, in other words, had been taken for granted. Now, I found solace in our post-diagnosis expressions of appreciation for each other. My last words to Joe could so easily have been a careless reminder to wipe the stove when he finished eating his eggs. Instead, my last words to him had been an expression of pride in how he'd handled illness—an echo of the admiration I'd expressed constantly during his years of treatment. Even more consoling were Joe's endgame expressions of gratitude for the efforts I'd made on his behalf, not only during his illness, but throughout our marriage. Joe left me feeling seen and appreciated. He'd conveyed that he understood not only how much I loved him, but also how often I'd put "us" before "me" during our twenty-seven years together. That meant a lot to me during my darkest days. It still does now.

I had memory of an alternate scenario that threw into sharp relief how fortunate it was that Joe and I had shared a good goodbye. In 1982 when Joe and I first began our giddy, tumultuous affair, I was involved with another man. My inexcusable infidelity made for a bad breakup, capped by a final, angry gesture on my soon-to-be-ex's part, after which he severed all contact. I had injured someone I loved, but there was no way to apologize, seek forgiveness, or make amends. So, I talked to him constantly in my head, replaying incidents from our relationship, straining to justify my actions, trying to make him understand that I hadn't meant to hurt him. My guilt didn't subside for almost two years.

With Joe, I experienced no guilt. No remorse. No What Ifs, If

Onlys, or I Didn't Means. I knew that I'd given him my very best. Absent anger, denial, or regret, I was left with a grief that was profound, but uncomplicated. I loved Joe. I missed Joe. I yearned for Joe. Perhaps because of my bad breakup experience, I regarded this uncluttered sadness as a gift. *Mostly, I am free to be sad,* I wrote seven weeks after Joe's death. *We expressed our love. We fought our fights and settled them . . . I guess the grief is "pure."* At least that's what Lynn and Ann say when I wonder why I'm not collapsing and hiding under the sheets.

The idea of a pure grief unencumbered by unfinished business had appeared in none of the grief-related books I'd read three years prior to Joe's diagnosis in preparation to write a novel (bizarrely, about a bereaved family grappling with the death of a loved one following a failed organ transplant). It also found no support in Bonanno's work or my initial conversations with the widows and widowers I'd approached or secured introductions to soon after Joe's death, looking to gain a sense of what lay ahead. As I'd mentioned to my attorney, Grace, two had told me, "It takes five years to get over your grief." What I hadn't mentioned to Grace was my unspoken—and ineloquent—thought in both instances: *No fucking way.* My life had been in a sort of suspended state during the two and a half years that Joe and I had dealt with his health. The thought of being suspended in a state of grief for five more agitated me.

When Grace had suggested a gentler scenario in which life went on, I'd asked, "Do you think that your long caretaking of your daughter helped prepare you for bereavement?"

Her first response was a look of surprise. "I never considered the possibility," she said. Then, after a moment's reflection, she nodded. "Yes," she said. "I think it did."

A student in the yoga class I joined after Joe's death would rein-
force that idea. Widowed a year, Laura helped ease my dread that
debilitating stages of grief were lying in wait. Like me, she'd enjoyed
a long and loving marriage. Like me, she'd taken care of her husband
through years of on-again-off-again sickness, yet had been stunned
when he died. Also like me, her grief didn't involve dredging up old
arguments to have the final word; licking old psychic wounds in need
of healing; kicking herself for having failed to express her love ade-
quately. She, too, was experiencing grief as an unmuddled sadness
that allowed room for lighter feelings. Laura told me that she never
lost her ability to take pleasure in her grown children's company; to
find distraction in yoga classes and dance; to mine enjoyment from
trips to her beach house and time spent with friends.

Over several lunches, Laura and I discovered we shared a belief
that because we'd been compelled to "think the unthinkable"
during our husbands' illnesses, we'd gained subconscious preparation for widowhood. We hypothesized that unlike people who
lose loved ones suddenly to heart attacks or tragic accidents, we'd
had the benefit of being forced by circumstance to contemplate the
possibility of loss and to grapple with our fears. Protracted periods
of caregiving had provided each of us with the opportunity to step
back from our daily lives and focus on our husbands. We'd had
time to air issues that needed discussing and share memories of
happier times. We'd also had the opportunity to give wholly of
ourselves to our spouses; to take stock of how much our husbands
meant to us; to put that love into words. All of this, we both felt in
hindsight, had been a gift.

"Jill, I think you are doing amazingly well," Laura wrote in an
e-mail three months after Joe's death. "Everyone said that to me,
also. I think we are very lucky we had the relationships that we
did, with no regrets, other than the fact that we don't have them
anymore."

I didn't require the benefit of other people's experience to know who was most responsible for holding despair at bay. Though only fifteen, my daughter absorbed the shock of her father's death with a maturity and calm that demanded no less of me.

Becky has always had an uncanny ability to step back from difficult situations and take stock. Hours after she came into our lives in Nanjing, Joe and I decided to give her a bath. Stripping off her mismatched orphanage clothes, we plunked her in the large hotel bathroom tub. Inexperienced and giddy, we made a mess of it, repeatedly dropping the soap as we held her upright. Despite the unfamiliarity of our faces, our touch, our language, and the sights and smells surrounding her, Becky accepted our inept ministrations with regal bearing, her eyes moving from Joe to me with a calm look that said, *Come on, people, get it together.* Laughing, I said to Joe, "I've never seen such a non-neurotic child. Our job is going to be not to fuck her up." Over the years, that has proved no joke.

Immediately following her dad's death, Becky exhibited characteristic composure, setting the tone for how we would cope. After we returned home from Pennsylvania, just hours after she'd seen her father slumped in a kitchen chair, dead, it became apparent that Becky wanted and needed to be surrounded by her friends. During the day, a constant crowd of teens congregated in the basement playroom; at night, one or another of her girlfriends camped out in her bedroom. Though grateful for the distraction and support they provided, I was concerned that Becky and I hadn't talked about Daddy's death and her feelings of grief.

A few days into our free-range shiva, I detected an opening. Knocking on her bedroom door, I found Becky alone on her bed, typing on her laptop. "I just had an odd experience," I said, then described how I'd thought I'd seen Daddy approaching the kitchen, only to discover it was Uncle Jonathan. "I guess we're going to have a lot of moments like that," I said, my tone open-ended, pitched to invite her to share any unusual experiences she might be having.

Instead, Becky looked up from her computer screen, said, "We'll cross that when we come to it," then turned back to the screen.

Pure Becky. Even-keeled. Ungiven to creating drama. Preternaturally able to remain clear-headed in the face of chaos or crisis. My instinct was to take her cue. If she wasn't ready to talk, I didn't want to push. Whatever she was feeling, she apparently felt more comfortable at the moment sharing it with her friends. To me, she gave her strength. From me, she clearly wanted the same. She'd just offered a very good reminder to stay in the moment and not get ahead of myself, projecting into a void that promised only to devour me. Becky's steadiness demanded that I remain steady, too. So, I did. It is very difficult to indulge your inner drama queen when your teenage daughter insists on behaving like an adult.

In coming months, I let Becky's level-headed approach guide me, remembering her words as Joe lay on the floor in our Pennsylvania kitchen: "I'm most worried about you. It upsets me more to see you crying than to see Daddy that way." Trusting an instinctive sense that she most needed me to maintain my composure, I saved my tears for when I was alone. I wanted neither to provoke her distress nor to give her cause for alarm. And I could empathize with her preference to see me behaving much as I always had. I remembered how Joe's initial upset following his diagnosis had stirred fear in me that I might have to fight what lay ahead alone. I had needed him to be the strong, determined Joe I'd always counted on. Becky, I felt, similarly needed the familiar Mom she knew in order to navigate the changed landscape of our lives.

That decision didn't spare me worry. Was my daughter repressing her pain? Wallowing in denial? Not processing her grief? Was my dry-eyed approach causing her to hold back potentially cathartic tears? Perhaps because Joe and I had come late to parenthood (he was fifty-two; I was thirty-nine) and our journey had been laborious (his resistance, our infertility, adoption's labyrinthine ways), we had shared an unflagging fascination with all things Becky. We would talk about her late into the night, giggling over amusing things she had said, discussing her development, and debating our parenting choices. Now, Joe's silence about Becky hit harder than any other aspect of his absence.

Early on, I asked Becky if she'd like to talk with a grief counselor. She responded that she'd rather talk with Lynn, who she knew was a clinical psychologist, and whom she knew, period. After she and Lynn went for a walk, Lynn reassured me that Becky was doing fine. Though I got a similar read from another psychologist friend whom Becky knew as one of the crew moms, I remained concerned. I had read so many press accounts (hell, I had written plenty myself) about traumatic situations where grief counselors had been rushed in to help teens deal with their grief. In Becky's case, not only was there no counselor, there was no outward display of grief. One of the few times she showed upset was when I suggested telling her teachers, at the start of the school year, about Dad's death. "That's stupid," she said adamantly. "I don't want their pitying looks." Who was I to argue with that?

Once again, it was Bonanno who came to my rescue. "Bereaved children tend to show about the same frequency of resilience as bereaved adults," he wrote in *The Other Side of Sadness*. "I've heard innumerable stories of well-meaning family and friends who've pressured otherwise healthy people to seek professional help so that they'll 'get in touch' with their hidden grief. The fact is that most of the time, there is no hidden grief." Moreover, he wrote, it is an "empirical fact that most bereaved people get better on their own, without any kind of professional help." After reading that, I stopped wondering if Becky should be in counseling.

Still, I continued to worry that my dry-eyed approach might warp her for life. Not yet confident as a single parent, I turned to friends for counsel. Several suggested that showing Becky my upset would be a "healthy invitation" for her to let down her own guard. Some went further, advising it was "important" for me to cry in front her so that she knew it was okay to cry. Though that made sense, it didn't feel right. Ultimately, it was a conversation with my friend Beth that convinced me to let Becky be Becky. More than any other friend's parenting style, Beth's accepting, unhovering approach had always resonated with me. Through the years, she'd been my go-to person for input on those few occasions when Joe and I were divided over some parenting issue. Her response? "Becky's already had one pillar pulled out. Seeing you upset might make her feel another pillar is teetering."

Case closed.

During the two weeks that people flowed in and out of my house, bringing consolation, distraction, and support, the one thing they didn't bring was any "Hey, you remember the time?" stories about Joe. My own mentions of Wease could freeze a friend's expression or set off a round of meaningful looks that people seemed to think I didn't see. A widow of new acquaintance told me she'd had the same experience right after her husband's death a year earlier. Even now, she said angrily, "People act as if he never existed." I found the silence bewildering until I grasped that people felt uneasy talking about Joe, for fear it might upset me. Though nothing could have been further from the truth, I had to make do with the reminiscences of Joe's college friends, who'd been eager to pool their memories. The stories were hilarious, but they predated my own memories of Joe.

The one obvious opportunity to share Joe stories was a memorial service. Joe had been clear that he wanted one. Because a prolonged autopsy was holding up his burial, I knew I had time to consider my options. Then, Becky tentatively expressed interest in going on a two-week camping trip she'd been looking forward to for months. The wilderness excursion, sponsored by a Y camp she'd attended the previous five summers, involved girls who were summer family for her. I nudged her to go, assuring her that Daddy's memorial service could wait.

The upside was that this gave me plenty of time to hone a list of speakers, write my own eulogy, and draw up a guest list that I hoped didn't overlook anyone. The downside was that it left me facing too much time to contemplate venues and menus. I'm a reluctant hostess at best. During my years with Joe, one of his few running complaints had been that we didn't entertain enough. My usual response was, "You want to throw a party? Fine. You do the inviting. You do the shopping. You do the cooking. I'll be happy to clean up." Now, I faced hosting the most meaningful gathering since our wedding—only this time without Joe's help or anchoring presence. The prospect filled me with a dread that grew as Ann and I visited various local rental facilities, each too impersonal to feel right.

Late one afternoon, our country friends swooped in en masse to pay their respects. Some had driven all the way from Pennsylvania; others had come from their weekday homes in Manhattan and New Jersey. A large crowd was milling in the dining room—noshing, natch—when the subject of Joe's memorial service came up. I recounted what Joe had said he wanted, including his crack about not wanting the service "overrun with Smolowes." I shared the meager results of my scouting trips with Ann, but not my jitters.

That would have been redundant. These were the people Joe and I had partied with most frequently over the years. My preference to work the cleanup shift rather than host was no secret.

"We'll do it," said Ken, Becky's godfather. He looked over at Arthur, Becky's other godfather, who responded with a nod.

"No." I shook my head. "I can't ask you to do that."

"You didn't," Ken said. "I offered."

At that point his partner, Arthur, joined in, saying they would hold the service at their (gorgeous) home in nearby Maplewood and take of care of the food preparations.

"I'll help," said a friend. "Me, too," said another. And another.

With that, not only was the weight of the memorial service miraculously lifted from my shoulders, but so, too, was any worry that the gathering might be unworthy of Joe. With Ken and Arthur in charge, I knew it would be tasteful. Elegant. Perfect.

I burst into tears. I had just experienced what it means to be overwhelmed by gratitude.

The shiva crowd exited first. Then, my siblings. Then, Becky.

On my own for the first time since Joe's death, I was wary of how I would handle so much empty time. *I've been tentative in my thinking about how I'm doing,* I wrote fifteen days after Joe's death. *I'm so aware that people will fade back into their lives. That I'm going to be alone for the next two weeks.* Usually I treasure alone time. Now I was concerned that so much solitude might sink me into depression.

Taking to heart advice offered by three different people who'd each buried a spouse—"If you don't want to do it, don't"—I tried to be gentle with myself and not do things because I thought I "should" or because I thought they would be "good" for me. When people extended invitations to concerts or dinners, I declined. I didn't want to be a drag on social gatherings; I also didn't want to have to feign enjoyment. Instead, my first move was to return to my job at *People*. Some friends and colleagues expressed concern that this choice might be premature, but I knew myself. Nothing engages my concentration more completely than writing. If I had to focus on producing a story on deadline, I would be forced to disrupt my thoughts about Joe.

The years of taking care of Joe had also taught me that I draw energy from conversations and activities that silence my anxious thoughts and help me to zero in on something other than myself. Now, I actively sought out diversion. *I try to plan something for every day, something that will get me out of the house and out of my head.* I scheduled walks with friends whom I knew I could count on not to dwell on my feelings of grief. I watched movies. I scheduled visits from my father, my older brother, and the West Coast college friend who throughout Joe's illness had made me laugh. To give Becky and me something to look forward to, I accepted an invitation from another college friend to visit her in the Bay Area in August.

That still left far too many unfilled hours. For years, I'd been getting out of bed around 4:00 a.m. to work without interruption on my long-term writing projects. Now, I was still waking up before dawn, but I had no interest in resuming work on my novel about a bereaved family, and I lacked the creative energy to start something new. I also lacked the concentration to read other people's novels. So my early morning habits changed. No longer concerned about disturbing a sleeping partner, I turned on the light and did whatever felt diverting. I answered e-mails. Read magazine and newspaper articles. Did crossword puzzles. Discovered Spider Solitaire on my laptop. As my bed turned into my predawn workstation, I gradually began to value the luxury of being able to do whatever I wanted, whenever I wanted.

With the start of the school year, I resumed my habit of making Becky breakfast and developed a new one: driving her to school. Until Joe's death, I'd insisted that she walk the damn mile. (In Joe, she'd always found an easier target for a ride.) Now, I had little stomach for our early-morning skirmishes, finding it less hassle to drive her than to repeatedly remind her that she was running late. To my surprise, I began to take pleasure in our carpooling runs.

Once up, however, my bed no longer appealed. Each day presented the same challenge: What now? Physical activity helped. So after cleaning out Joe's bedroom closet and drawers, I tackled the attic, going through his mountains of boxes. At times I wondered if my rush to discard was callous. Later, two widowers told me they began the same process within days of their wives' deaths. A widow told me the first thing she did after her husband died was discard her sheets and quilt and purchase new bedding. Being left behind isn't easy; you do what you have to do. If nothing else, all that sifting, piling, re-boxing, recycling, and discarding provided moments of distraction from my grief.

As I sorted through box after box, I culled out final drafts of Joe's novel and two full-length plays for Becky; Treen family letters, photos, and memorabilia for Esme; items I thought would have personal meaning for his close friends whom I'd asked to speak at the memorial service. For an undesignated audience—me? Becky?—I set aside Joe's voluminous collection of journalism clips and journals, his assorted diplomas and yearbooks, his old electric typewriter, and long-forgotten cache of framed wall hangings. Then, per his instructions, I began discarding the rest. Each time I lugged another heavy box down the two flights of stairs to the ground floor, I muttered something affectionate like, "Goddamn you, Wease. You gotta fucking be kidding me." After several weeks of this, my interest gave out.

There are still untouched boxes in need of hauling. (*Jesus, Wease.*

More?) But Joe had given me a gift. By itemizing what I should save and telling me, "Everything else, throw it away," he'd given me license to purge. Absent that blessing, I would have hesitated and not discovered that with all those receipts, tax records, writing drafts, research books, and faded reporter notebooks gone, the weight of his presence—or absence—had lightened a bit.

Each day, I continued to draw solace from the appreciation Joe had expressed throughout his illness and then again shortly before his death. One day as I worked on my tribute for Wease, it occurred to me that too often such sentiments are saved for eulogies. I wanted the friends, relatives, and colleagues whose kindness had particularly touched or steadied me over the last few years to know what I valued most about their support. Now. Before it was too late.

So, I began writing thank-you letters, not casual notes of acknowledgment, but heartfelt expressions of gratitude. I wanted— no, I needed—to give clear expression to what exactly it was about each person's support that had lightened my load during the years of Joe's illness and was continuing to buttress me in the wake of his death. At one level, this was a writing challenge that distracted me from painful thoughts of Joe. At a deeper level, it was an existential challenge that demanded I pay attention to the blessings in my life. Each time I uncorked my gratitude and let it flow, it helped me recognize the many reasons I had to go on without Joe.

I don't remember the particulars of any given note, but I know one key thing I didn't share with anyone, because it didn't occur to me until I was well into the writing of this book. As I revisited the gestures of kindness and particular types of support that had helped me, trying to identify ever more closely what had been most useful during Joe's illness, I realized something that, once it presented itself, seemed both obvious and important.

In the days following Joe's diagnosis, I had instinctively resolved not to be hemmed in by people's concern and shut out from the rest of life. As a result, I'd gravitated to people who accepted that I didn't want to talk about Joe's illness and its toll. Month after month, as these friends continued to fill my mind with other ideas, I came to appreciate that they were providing something more than a respite from my static state of worry. All those walks and talks with the women in my writers' group who kept me abreast of their writing frustrations were helping me to maintain a connection to the creative part of my life. The challenging stories my *People* editors assigned me—rather than trying to placate me with mindless busywork—were enabling me to continue functioning as a journalist. And the friends who, taking me at my word, pushed past resistant thoughts of "I don't want to burden Jill with my problems" to talk about their financial strains, their less-than-perfect marriages, their parenting dilemmas—in short, their lives—were helping me not only to still feel like a valued friend, but to keep my own woes in perspective.

But it wasn't until two years after Joe's death that another dividend—the most important one—came into focus. New widowhood, I realized, would have been a lot more difficult and lonely if I'd emerged from the isolation of Joe's protracted medical crisis to discover my other relationships had so atrophied that all that remained of my life were my memories of Joe. Instead, my life was still rich with engaging, caring relationships. Because there had been give-and-take all along, I was as familiar with the twists and turns of my friends' lives as they were with mine. They were active and present in my life; I was active and present in theirs. Had my travails dominated conversation from Joe's diagnosis to his death, perhaps that imbalance would have curbed people's desire to spend time with me. (Jill is like a broken record.) Bred resentment. (She's not the only one with problems.) Damaged intimacy. (Why would I turn to Jill? All we ever do is talk about her.) Even if the constant focus on me hadn't felt narrowing or skewed to them, it would have to me, out of sync with the sorts of relationships I'd enjoyed prior to Joe's illness. Instead, though circumstance had put a cloud over my head that none of us could ignore, my friendships had remained alive and vibrant. In some cases, they'd even deepened.

No, I didn't have to reimagine my life. Save for Joe, the relationships that had always given my days richness and texture were still intact and recognizable. I didn't have to reimagine my life, I realized, because, thank God, I still had one.

10

SERENDIPITY

As we climbed into a hotel bed on our wedding night, Joe asked me, "Did you read the inscription in your ring?" Unaware that Joe had engraved it, I slipped the band off my finger and angled the interior under the bedside light: *J.S. & J.M.T. 4-21-85.*

"What are you doing?" Joe gasped. "You can't take that off!" I looked at him, surprised and more than a little charmed.

"Here," I said, handing him the ring. "Put it back on my finger and I'll never take it off again."

For the next twenty-four years, I honored that pledge. Except for the two occasions when swollen fingers necessitated that I have it enlarged, the gold band never left my finger. I loved that ring. Because there'd been no need for matching unisex bands (Joe, who hated the feel of rings, had decided not to wear one), I'd been free to pick a piece of jewelry that I liked. More important, I loved what the ring represented.

But in the weeks leading up to the three-month anniversary of Joe's death, the ring began to feel uncomfortable. *It has felt increasingly dishonest . . . It sends a message to others: I'm married. I'm not. I'm single. I'm a widow. I hate it.*

Shortly after midnight on the three-month anniversary of Joe's death, I took off my wedding band. This time, when I angled it beneath the bedside light, I discovered that one of those ring enlargements had abbreviated the inscription to "M.T. 4-21-85," the rest erased, as Joe had been erased from my life. I sobbed that night. The next morning, I opened my jewelry box, removed a gold link bracelet that Joe had given me, and fastened it around my right wrist. But it wasn't the same. (Nor will it ever be, though I've yet to remove it and expect to die with it still on my wrist.) For days I couldn't stop looking at my naked finger, dented by a phantom band, which remains to this day. *A ring marks your place in the universe. You are someone who is loved, accounted for, attached. An empty finger says you are alone.*

Now, a feeling of aloneness settled over me that was distinct from my grief, coloring everything in much the way that worry had tinted my days for the last two and a half years. From high school on, I'd almost always been part of a couple. This didn't speak to a need for some guy to direct my life; to the contrary, I prefer making and acting upon my own decisions. Instead, my strong inclination to partner stemmed from a bedrock certainty—fostered, no doubt, by the delight my parents took in one another's company throughout my childhood—that life was richer and more enjoyable when shared. The prospect of spending the rest my life alone felt unbearable.

Loving an absence is very different from loving a presence . . . Who will talk to me? Who will listen to me? Who will care whether I come home at the end of the day? Who will be so easy with me that we can be comfortable together no matter what we're doing, or probably more to the point, no matter what we're not doing? . . . If there's no companion, where does the love I want to give find a home?

One night during this period a friend invited me to an impromptu barbecue. I arrived to find four couples who were clearly accustomed to socializing together. I'd approached the dinner feeling grateful for the invitation; recently, a widow had told me how much she resented no longer being invited to "couples' dinners." But when conversation turned to where each married pair was thinking of relocating after their kids left for college, I began to wish I hadn't come. Joe and I had entertained this "Where will we retire?" conversation countless times. We'd even identified a few candidates over the years: the Cayuga Lake area in upstate New York, Escondido in California, Albuquerque in New Mexico. The couples' conversation made me weary with loneliness. Pleading work, I slipped away, got in my car, and bawled.

Soon after I got home, the mother of one of Becky's friends pulled up to retrieve her daughter. "You okay?" she asked, peering anxiously at my tear-stained face. When I recounted the conversation that had triggered the waterworks, her face tightened with judgment. "How inconsiderate," she said. But I didn't feel that way. They were just couples being couples, each set of spouses relaxed and comfortable and certain that they would face the future as a pair. How could I begrudge them that happiness? It was what I had always wanted. What I had shared with Joe. What I still wanted.

Over the next month, I began to think about meeting men, an idea that didn't sit comfortably. *I don't think it's disrespectful of Joe. To the contrary, I think it's a testament to our marriage. Our marriage made me happy. Very happy. Why wouldn't I want to experience such happiness again?* Then again, *I am not fit for dating at present. I would just be looking for someone to fill Joe's shoes.*

At the same time, other aspects of my life were whittling away at my ambivalence. I was growing impatient with the widow role, the somber chorus of "How *are* you?" that greeted me at every turn, the winces of concern that creased people's faces when they spotted me. Far more disturbing, just three months after losing Joe, my sister's cancer prognosis had taken a grim turn. Already, too many phone calls with Ann were ending with the wrenching thought that some day in the not-nearly-distant-enough future I would dial her home number and she would no longer be there to take my call. I needed to put my hands on something that reintroduced happiness into my life and offered hope of a future not steeped in sorrow.

But how? Where? With whom? A gazillion years ago when I'd last dated, I'd met men primarily in the workplace. That was now a nonstarter. After three rounds of layoffs at *People*, most of the men my age or older were gone. The guys on my floor looked like kids to me. I didn't even want to think what sort of dinosaur I looked like to them. Over the years, I'd read about online dating, never once imagining it might ever touch my life. Now, I randomly snatched a name out of the ethersphere—Match.com—and logged on to see how it worked, only to discover that I had to sign up for a free three-day trial to access the site.

I signed up and crafted a brief profile, sans photo, that showed traces of humor, but included a pointed Not Available clause: "Recently widowed, I'm more interested in male companionship than romance at the moment." After a few responses trickled in, I wrote, *The match.com stuff just makes me feel more alone . . . I don't actually want to date any of these guys. I just want reassurance there's a future out there somewhere.* That afternoon when I logged on to remove my profile from the site, there was a witty message from a man whose profile showed evidence of humor and intelligence. A night later after a flurry of comical e-mails, we spoke by phone. It was clear from the get-go this man wasn't my type. But Lord, how this guy could make me laugh. Clever and bawdy, Mr. Hilarity was just what I needed. Each of the next six nights, I stood on the back porch, phone in one hand, a glass of wine in the other, laughing myself silly. Each of the next six mornings, I awoke to doubt. *This morning I was apologizing to Joe in my head, asking myself why am I doing this, and the answer came back: survival.*

Thinking I needed affirmation—though I now see what I was

really seeking was permission—I ran the idea of dating past my two younger siblings. Ann said, "Go for it." Jonathan said, "I think it's great that you're trying to jumpstart your life." Using an e-mail address that didn't disclose my identity, I also e-mailed George Bonanno, my self-designated bereavement guru. "I recently read your new book with great interest and admiration. Widowed four months after a very happy 24-year marriage . . . this is uneasy for me to admit: I already feel an inclination to date. I'm wondering if this is unusual . . . My sadness is with me all the time; but so is the desire to look toward a future."

"It is actually very common for people to mourn a loved one but at the same time wish to move on," he wrote back. "I think we are wired to do that. The only problem seems to be when we worry too much that it is somehow not appropriate."

His words of support helped. But it was Lynn's response that proved the real game-changer. "You haven't been grieving for just four months," she told me. "You've been grieving since the day Joe was diagnosed." That felt exactly right.

Mr. Hilarity, however, did not. Our first date at a bowling alley (his suggestion) would also be our last. It wasn't because I could feel his eyes on my ass each time I bent to launch the ball down the lane. (I actually got a kick out of that.) It also wasn't because I knew we had no future; I knew that before we met. Rather, it was the realization that I wasn't ready to date; it was unfair to lead this nice man on.

I ended my brief flirtation with both him and the world of online matchmaking, yet I came away heartened by the experience. I'd done it, I'd taken my first tentative baby step toward a someday future without Joe. Cyber-dating, with its progression of e-mails and phone calls, had proved more appealing than the prospect of being set up on a blind date, only to find myself stuck with a boor or bore for a three-hour dinner. I'd also emerged from my one date a bit savvier. When we met, Mr. Hilarity's first surprised words had been, "You look just like your picture." Until that moment it hadn't occurred to me that people might lie about all manner of things in their profiles. Most important, my anxiety that I might never meet anybody ever again had quieted. *For all my fear of being alone to the end of my life, there is a thrall, a hope, that there is a new life out there for me and that I can't imagine what it will be.*

Over the next two months I found ways, old and new, to fill my hours. I learned to use a digital camera. Boxed up stacks of Joe's books for a high school fundraiser. Had my bedroom repainted and recarpeted. Converted Joe's upstairs office into mine after the installation of an indoor oil tank left my basement lair smelling of fumes. Played endless rounds of Spider Solitaire. Raked and bagged fall leaves. Learned how to use the snow blower, once Joe's toy. Weekdays I looped the park at a fast pace, the music on my iPod ratcheted up to crowd out my thoughts. Saturday mornings I attended yoga classes.

Somewhere in there, I broached the subject of dating with Becky, who was now in tenth grade. "You are *so* not ready to date," she said. When will I be? "After I leave for college." Almost three years from now? I didn't know whether to laugh or cry. For a few days I soaked in guilt. Forget my own reservations, how could I do this to my daughter? Then I recognized that for the indulgence it was. Joe and I had always shared the view that our primary job as parents was to prepare Becky to go out into the world (then hope like hell she'd come back to visit because she wanted to, not because she felt she had to). The last thing I wanted for her now was to feel tethered to me out of a sense of concern or obligation.

A few days later, Becky offered a reprieve. "You can date, but

I don't want to wake up and discover someone in your bed." No problem. Even I couldn't imagine that. Not yet.

Late that November, I mentioned to a friend that I was starting to think about dating. She relayed my words to a mutual friend, who shot me an e-mail: "Is it true you are ready to date??"

"I just want to get out," I typed back. "Sitting home breeds dismal thoughts."

Though my words suggested confidence, I was anything but. Those double-barreled question marks reinforced my concern that I might unintentionally inflict pain on friends and family who felt I was being disrespectful of Joe's memory. *Was* I being disrespectful? Joe's blessing to move on had been offered without a timeframe. Though Lynn's "You've been grieving since the day Joe was diagnosed" had stilled my qualms, it hadn't erased my hesitation.

The final push was provided by what should have been an unmemorable event: a colonoscopy. Ann's diagnosis had prompted my doctor to accelerate my testing schedule from a five-year to a two-year rotation. The local hospital required that someone else do the driving after the anesthesia wore off. I didn't mind so much that my friend Pamela, rather than Joe, shuttled me home. But when I came through the kitchen door, it suddenly hit me—hard. *No one to share the results with. No Wease. It just feels so alone. Like who gives a shit (so to speak)?* Dissolving into noisy sobs, I realized the time had come to act.

At the mid-December meeting of the Montclair Writers Group, we honored our year-end tradition of hoisting glasses of champagne and offering brief statements about our professional and personal goals for the year ahead. When it came my turn, I said I wanted to get back to writing. Applause. On the personal side, I said, I wanted to start dating. That drew enthusiastic gasps. Yes! She's getting on with her life!

Upholding another annual tradition, Becky and I spent New

Year's in Pennsylvania, but this holiday season we stayed at her godfathers' home. I wasn't ready yet to reopen our own house. While I had a life in Montclair that involved activities and relationships independent of Joe, every aspect of my country existence was inextricably connected to Wease. We'd cultivated every friendship and flowerbed together. We'd developed our pastimes—mountain biking, cross-country skiing, snowshoeing—together. We'd chosen every rug and every wall hanging together. Returning to the kitchen where Joe had died was more than I wanted to handle.

On New Year's Day 2010, I slipped off to an untrafficked room with my laptop and signed up on two sites for six months of dating. A canvass of both sites quickly made clear I was not what anyone might call a romantic. People who prioritized "walks on the beach" and "candlelit dinners" held no appeal. To my mind, people who write stuff like that not only suffer from hackneyed thinking, but also lack a realistic sense of what it takes to create a lasting relationship. I also turned away from men who spoke of searching for a "soul mate." The way I see it, marriage is as much a function of timing as finding the "right" mate. I'd enjoyed several wonderful relationships before I met Joe, two of which might have ended at the altar had they come at a different moment in my life. I had no interest in men who were counting on fate to make and sustain a relationship.

I was, however, interested in connecting with men whose profiles offered hints of the characteristics I considered essential, what Lynn called my "non-negotiables." Years of premarital dating had honed my list. Years of marriage had further culled that list to the qualities that had enlivened my relationship with Joe in good times and helped hold us together during difficult patches. For my wish list, I wrote: "Essentials: compromise, mutual trust, laughter and lively dialogue . . . Enhancers: affection, intelligence, ardor, appreciation, a good sense of humor, the ridiculous, and himself . . .

Gut-level belief: life is sweeter when shared." About myself, I wrote: "A veteran journalist, I'll introduce myself by way of five Ws: Warm (but not fuzzy) . . . Witty (but not snarky) . . . Word-driven (passions: reading, writing, crosswords, intelligent conversation) . . . Well-grounded (ungiven to drama)...Widowed (after a happy 24-year marriage)."

For me, that last *W* was the most critical. I wanted men to know I'd been happily married; if it scared someone off, he probably wasn't my kind of guy. Moreover, while I was open to meeting divorced men (though not guys who'd never married—to my mind that raised too many commitment questions), my preference was for a widower with a happy marriage in his past. Any guy who'd been in a longstanding marriage wouldn't come wearing blinders; he'd know that it requires work to keep a relationship fresh and engaging. If death, not choice, had ended his marriage, there was a good chance that he, like I, missed having someone with whom to share life's ups and downs.

I had some other unstated preferences of the nonessential variety. I'd always dated journalists and had been married to one. This time round, I thought it might be interesting to meet a man whose career was different from mine. Though I was willing to schlep into Manhattan, I preferred to keep things on my side of the Hudson River. Finally, with retirement ahead, I favored someone who wanted to travel and envisioned a lot of togetherness. Joe and I had learned to navigate our whose-time-is-more-valuable issues, but it had taken years.

After attaching a photo that I hoped looked friendly, I clicked the send button on two profiles, then returned to the New Year's festivities, too red-faced to admit what I'd been doing. In coming days, my embarrassment dissolved as I enjoyed the flurry of attention that comes with being a newbie on a dating site. I struck up a correspondence with a widowed attorney who'd just lost his wife after a prolonged illness and seemed in need of reassurance that it was okay for him to be venturing online. I had a flirty exchange with a musician that went up in smoke when he came across as a curmudgeon on the phone. I entertained humorous e-mail repartee with a divorced doctor in his early seventies, only to discover, when he suggested that we meet, that I found his age a barrier. I'd done a lot of caregiving in recent years and didn't want to revisit that situation anytime soon. I had lunch with a divorced guy, and as I prepared for dinner with another divorcé felt heartened when Becky offered to help me put together an outfit. Both meals were enjoyable; neither stirred feelings deeper than relief to be venturing forward.

On a Sunday night ten days into my new cyber life, I received a message: "I'm a recent widower, living in South Orange. Your profile is intriguing. Would you be interested in a chat or perhaps a cup of coffee?" When I punched up his profile, I felt no attraction to his stiff picture, and his mention (twice) of a soul mate made me wince. But other aspects of his write-up definitely appealed. Lines like "I need to be a fully involved half of a wonderful whole. I want to share my life" and "Mutual respect and an ability to compromise are essential" echoed my own priorities. He was a water engineer. I'd never met, let alone dated, an engineer. He lived on my side of the bridge-and-tunnel traffic and was only six years older. Of particular note, in the "Ideal relationship" section he'd written, "That's difficult for me to describe. I was happily married to a dear woman for 38 years. She was bright, sassy and always fun to be with." I liked that he'd had a long, happy marriage. I liked that he'd loved his wife. I liked that in putting himself forward, he felt it important that women know those two things about him.

"A phone chat sounds delightful," I wrote back.

I had to work late the next night and my January writers' group meeting was scheduled for the night after that. So, we settled on Wednesday at 8:00 p.m. "Looks like we'll find plenty to talk about," I wrote as we wound down our exchange. "Don't know if you're willing to go there, but I'm interested in how long you've been widowed, how you're doing, etc. Don't know too many people in a situation similar to mine (widowed after a long, happy marriage) . . . I'm sure we'll figure it out as we go. Look forward to chatting. jill"

To my surprise, he wrote right back. "Hi, Jill. I lost my darling wife in April. She was diagnosed with lung cancer six weeks earlier. We were college sweethearts." As I read on that Leslie had been "a voracious reader and a crossword puzzle fanatic" and, for a time, a journalist, an alarm went off in my brain: was this guy hoping to find a stand-in for Leslie? After sharing some information about his work and his two grown children, who were on either side of thirty, he signed off, "Bob."

Two nights later there was an e-mail waiting when I got home. "I just want to say hello before bed." After a brief back-and-forth, I typed "sleep tight," then, thinking that too cozy, substituted, "'night." Bob responded, "8:00 p.m. Don't be late! Sweet dreams." Awww. "I'll be here," I answered. "Sleep tight." Charmed, I called up his profile again and discovered some additions. "Just to put it out there, I cannot dance. I have two left feet and no sense of rhythm. But I know for sure I can make a woman happy." He'd also filled in the "I'm looking for" section: "A partner, a companion, someone with whom to share experiences, both good and bad, a best friend, a lover, an advocate, a defender, a princess." A princess? Earlier in my life, I would have gagged. Instead, I smiled. Despite his talk of a soul mate, this guy sounded like a realist; I particularly liked that part about "good and bad." If he wanted to put a woman on a pedestal, fine—so long as he was willing to share the stand.

Bob phoned five minutes ahead of schedule, as if to say, I couldn't wait. From the moment I answered, our conversation flowed. "You mentioned your daughter, Bex," I opened. "Is that short for Rebecca?" Yes, she'd grown up a Becky, then converted to Bex during her college years. As he talked about her career and shared a humorous story about one of her wilder escapades, what came through loudest was that this was a very proud and accepting dad. "My daughter's a Becky, too," I said. "But that wasn't her name at birth. She was born in China."

"I know," he said. "I know a lot of things about you." How was that possible? My e-mails hadn't mentioned my last name. "My daughter's a journalist."

I thought a second. "Reverse phone book?"

Bingo. It didn't bother me that he'd checked me out. I'd tried to do the same after he supplied an e-mail address that included his last name, only to discover countless guys with the same name. Instead, I was struck that he'd told his daughter about our date. Were his kids okay with his dating? He responded that he'd begun thinking about dating four months after his wife's death, but had held off, concerned about the effect it might have on his son and daughter. At Thanksgiving, he'd told them and gotten their approval; his mother and even his mother-in-law had been urging him to date. This sounded a lot like my own situation: a desire to move on; a need to seek permission from loved ones; an answering chorus of "Go for it."

When we segued into a discussion about dealing with grief, I was struck by both his candor and the similarities in our attitudes. Though we'd both had Jewish upbringings, neither of us had sought comfort in a congregation or a God. "I hear a lot of 'It's so unfair,'" I said. "I answer with a smile, but what I'm thinking is, Why is it unfair? It's sad. It's awful. But not unfair. It happens." Big agreement from Bob on that one. He also offered strong agreement when I said, "It's not my inclination to think, Why me? To me, the answer is, Why not me?" He told me that his grief came in waves and that work helped a lot. That sounded familiar.

Two hours flew by without either of us having to fall back on "What kind of books do you like?" or "What movies have you seen lately?" By the end, my voice was hoarse. "I'm just going to be blunt," I said. "I'd like to meet you." Yes, yes, he said, he wanted to meet me, too. Quickly, we settled on Saturday night. He would come to Montclair; I would select the restaurant.

The next morning I awoke with a Blood, Sweat & Tears song I hadn't thought of in decades playing in my head: "You've Made Me So Very Happy." *This guy doesn't sound too good to be true—he sounds true*, I wrote.

That night, in a second long conversation, I learned that at Bob's request his son had moved home after Leslie's death; that Bob loved to cook (and Leslie had hated the kitchen as much as I do); that this was a guy very on top of the news; that he had wide-ranging tastes in music; that he was a directional dyslexic (like me!); that he could drop the F-bomb with ease (also like me!). He answered my questions with confidence, but without arrogance. No subject seemed to faze him. *It's impossible not to feel warm about this man. He's openly warm, not afraid to talk about emotional stuff, worldly, intelligent, a fluid, humorous, wonderful conversationalist.*

Still, I had an uncomfortably superficial concern that I couldn't ignore. In the physical description section of his profile, Bob had checked the "few extra pounds" box. What did that mean exactly? Physically active myself, I've always been attracted to fit men. What if his weight was a turn off? The previous night he'd told me that he wanted to focus on me and had "hidden" his profile on the dating site. I'd protested that was premature. "This is part of what makes cyberdating so bizarre," I said. "Used to be you felt an attraction toward someone and then reached out to connect; here, you connect before you know if there's a natural attraction."

"I can't juggle six balls at a time, with my two left feet," he responded. "This is just something I need to do for myself." He didn't ask if I planned to follow suit. He simply moved on to another topic.

Hours before our dinner, my nervousness surged. By now, Bob and I knew a remarkable amount about each other, far more than a typical first date. *He wants this to work. So do I. Too much build-up here. I'm jittery, maybe that's the word. Jittery and restless. This feels like a "big" date.* As Becky helped me dress, she offered sane, mature advice. "Don't expect Daddy. Don't look for the same things as him." Damn, I have a canny kid.

I arrived at the Chinese restaurant first. When Bob walked through the door, my concerns about physical attraction evaporated. He was handsomer than his picture—his smile warm, his height appealing. Yes, he carried a few extra pounds, but he carried them well. I stood and greeted him with a hug. After we sat, he reached across the table. "I'm so nervous that I have to hold your hands," he said. Just like that. He made it so easy.

I don't remember what we ate. Actually, I don't remember eating at all. What I do remember is that we talked and talked without discomfort or restraint. Afterwards, I invited him back to my house. As we sat facing each other on the living room couch, the first hint of awkwardness set in.

"Should we just get this over with?" Bob asked.

I looked at him, relieved. "Yes, please."

It wasn't magical, our first kiss. It was reserved and tentative, a chaste acknowledgment that I wasn't Leslie, and Bob wasn't Joe. Rather than fanning the heat that had been building all evening, it reminded us that not all that long ago we'd each been committed, monogamous spouses who never expected or wanted to be in this situation. It was, in other words, just what it needed to be.

After Bob left, I sent him an e-mail. "Hope you got home without too many wrong turns. Me, I'm going to sleep feeling reassured that you feel like a very right turn in my life. 38 years, 27 years, those relationships are irreplaceable and have to be acknowledged and respected. After tonight, I feel about Leslie much the way I feel about Becky's birthmother: thank you so much for delivering such an amazing person into my life. Sleep tight."

"I am ecstatic that we 'connected,'" he wrote back. "I was petrified that we wouldn't. I'm feeling complete again. Thanks for being you. Sweet dreams."

Bypassing "Too much, too soon?" jitters, I removed my profile from the dating sites the next day. After it became clear that neither of us was looking to replicate either the marriage or the person we had lost, our relationship accelerated. Rapidly, we progressed from demure handholding to physical intimacy; from talk of "next weekend" to talk of "when we retire." Bob called our connection *bashert*, which he explained was Yiddish for "meant to be." Fate? I was more inclined to credit a less romantic explanation: profound loss had heightened our awareness and appreciation of what made each of us happy. Either way, after so much sorrow, neither Bob nor I were inclined to erect emotional roadblocks. Instead, we opened our arms wide to each other. *There have been so many years of heaviness, heartache, worry, pain, worrying about my future*, I wrote four days after our first date, a day when my inner DJ was spinning "Walking on Sunshine." *My inclination is to not resist the happiness. Just bathe in it. Enjoy.*

I knew a good case could be made that we were moving into

each other's lives with imprudent speed. But I also knew there was a reliable brake on our exuberance: my love for Becky would safeguard against the kinds of precipitous decisions I'd been cautioned no widow should make her first year. My daughter had endured enough change in her life, and in case I couldn't see that for myself, she let me know it soon after I introduced her to Bob.

"Oh, God," she said, with a cringe in her voice. "He's not going to move in here, is he?"

"Absolutely not. Nothing like that is going to happen until you go off to college."

It wouldn't be long before I felt a need to tell Bob the same. "You're absolutely right," he said. "You and Becky need this time together." He was willing to take our relationship at whatever pace I needed. He was ahead of me on only one point. Soon, Bob began dropping unfinished sentences. "There's something I want to tell you—" he offered. And, "I know I shouldn't use the *L* word—"

"Then don't," I said. "We don't know each other that well yet. And you know as well as I do that this giddy stuff isn't what makes a relationship go the distance." Forget about the *L* word, I suggested. "All of this is so unexpected and wonderful. Let's just enjoy being happy after so much pain."

Though my tone was playful, I really didn't want to hear it. I didn't want to think about it. I didn't want to feel pressured to say it. Maybe our romance would prove no more than an infatuation or a comforting interlude. Certainly a key part of what made us feel so right for each other was that we understood each other's pain. Our delight in one another's company did not spare either of us our sorrow, nor did either of us want it to. Grief was a constant presence in our lives and in our conversations. We traded stories about how we'd handled the post-death decisions, the loneliness, the concern of friends. We talked about the differences between the long walk-up to Joe's death and the all-too-short sprint from

Leslie's diagnosis to her death. We leveled with each other when we'd had a miserable day, and didn't feel slighted or threatened when the other needed time alone. Together, we discovered that it was possible to be happy and sad at the same time. That we could experience this seeming contradiction together, without need of apology or explanation, had helped us to forge a fast connection. But was this the glue that bound us? If so, was that what either of us wanted?

One evening about a month into our courtship, we were sitting in the living room, chatting and drinking wine, when I heard the lock turn in the kitchen door. I waited for the familiar sequence of settling sounds—sneakered footsteps on the wood floor, the thump of Becky's gym bag landing on the counter, the refrigerator door opening and closing—before calling out, "Bob and I are in the living room, sweetie."

Casual. Breezy. Just the sort of mundane scene that Joe would have exploited to brilliant comic effect in one of his stage plays. "Subtext, Wease, it's all in the subtext," he used to remind me when he felt something I'd written was overstated or gave away too much.

Now, I am laying the groundwork for Becky. I am in the living room. I am not alone. Bob is here. Subtext: I don't want you to be caught off-guard, sweetheart.

More footsteps, then Becky enters. If she'd come upon Bob and me a half hour earlier, she would have wanted to gouge her eyes out. Instead, she encounters a tame tableau, Bob and I seated chastely on a couch, Misty parked between us.

"Hi," Becky says, her eyes on Bob. "I feel bad that every time you see me, I'm dressed like this."

As she gestures at her sweats, I well with pride. Plainly, she is exhausted after a two-hour crew workout. More to the point, I know this isn't easy for my daughter. Joe's daughter. She could have opted to flee up the stairs to her bedroom, shouting, "Hi," behind her, as she'd done the few other times Bob had come by. Instead, she's chosen to join us and is making eye contact with Bob, her expression friendly—an invitation to chat.

"I was confused when I came in," she says. "I saw your car in the driveway and was, like, Whose Subaru is that? It looks like our car."

"Smaller model," Bob says agreeably.

"What was the workout today?" I ask.

Indoor erging. Two 5k circuits. "I was dying after the second one," she says.

"How do those rowing machines work?" Bob asks. How do they measure time? Distance? Force? "Can you feather the handle like you do with an oar?"

"Feather" the handle? Where the hell did that come from? I look at Bob admiringly. And look how easily he's engaging her, his manner relaxed and casual, friendly but not too eager. Just a wide-open target she can't miss.

For several minutes, they talk about rowing. Nothing momentous. Yet the subtext is deafening. I haven't experienced such subtlety since the day Dr. B uttered the word "leukemia" and opacity was stripped from my life. There is nothing subtle about leukemia. Nothing subtle about the fears a disease like that unleashes. Nothing subtle about the exhausting and exhaustive caregiving duties such an illness requires. When survival is on the line, your days, your priorities, your decisions are very black and white. You become adept at identifying precisely what you need, precisely what you feel, precisely what you must do to get yourself and your loved ones through the day. Because there is no time for subtle messages that you hope will eventually reach their mark, you become expert at transmitting transparent messages that help you meet the needs of the people you love. You learn to be honest, direct, concise. *Later,* you understand, is a luxury, not a given. So you become alert to what you have: *Here. Now.*

And in this new *here,* this new *now,* I am suddenly alert to the rich opaqueness that is reentering my life. I am alert to the deft way my new boyfriend is navigating my teenage daughter's conflicted sensibilities. I am alert to the strong feelings his gentle, open-hearted effort is stirring in me. After Becky politely excuses herself and heads upstairs to shower, I lean into Bob. Without forethought, without calculation, without subtext, I whisper, "I love you."

"Call me when you get home," I said as we parted that night. It was snowing. We'd been drinking wine. I wanted to know that Bob had made it home safely. As the minutes ticked past his usual twenty-minute commute—forty minutes, an hour—I began to worry. Then my mind made a leap, and I felt my stomach sink. *Not again.* And with that came another thought: *I'm glad I said it to him. If he were to go, I'd regret I hadn't.*

When the phone finally rang, Bob's first words were, "Did you mean what you said?"

"I love you, Bob," I repeated. During his prolonged drive home, I'd been reminded that waiting was a game of chance. Nothing in life is guaranteed. Our relationship was a gift.

So was its timing. By our first date, both my mother and my sister were in irreversible decline. The question of whether either of them was going to die had given way to three terrible new questions: How soon? Who first? How much physical agony would each of them suffer before she went? Already, fresh waves of sorrow were beginning to buffet me. I was well aware that Bob's presence in my life was providing a steadying and much-needed counterbalance.

He'd reintroduced happiness into my life. He held out hope of a brighter future.

What I didn't see, or rather what I took for granted, is rather stunning. Given the double emotional whammy headed my way, it would have been understandable for a man of such recent acquaintance, especially one grappling with his own grief, to bow out quickly. Far from being scared off, Bob moved in closer, making it clear that he wanted to provide support and comfort throughout the ordeal ahead. Remarkable as I find that in hindsight, that's not what amazes me. This is: though I'd known Bob barely a month, my trust in him already ran so deep that it never occurred to me, not once, to question or doubt that he would do just what he said he would do.

No wonder my inner DJ was in overdrive.

11

SOLACE

By the time I met Bob in January 2010, my brothers and I were referring to my sister's and mother's dual declines as their "race to the finish." Dad and I wanly called it "The Smolowe Curse." Mom's grim endgame was marked by punishing physical pain, dramatic weight loss, and yellowing skin—evidence that her liver was failing. There was no predicting how long this would go on. Her hospice workers thought it a wonder that she'd hung on so long.

Ann's days as a "miracle patient," meanwhile, had come to an abrupt halt three months after Joe's death when an MRI, taken four days in advance of scheduled liver resection surgery, showed that her existing tumors had grown and new ones had sprouted. The surgery called off, I wailed as I drove up to Vermont. Now, instead of my being her post-op watchdog, Ann wanted me to accompany her on her rounds of oncologists as she explored her options. Her husband, Jim, was "too upset to come," she said.

When I walked into their house, I encountered a painful scene: Ann tense, Jim shell-shocked, the two of them discussing her next step. Ann was adamant she didn't want more chemo, which to her mind promised more unpleasant side effects, but no hope of a cure or significantly more time. "I want to die with dignity," she said more than once. Jim, it emerged, wasn't "too upset" to participate in her consultations with doctors. Rather, he was trying to give Ann space to make her choices without his own feelings getting in the way.

"They're negotiating her death," Lynn said to me by phone.

As I listened to Ann and Jim struggle to find mutual ground, I realized Joe and I had had it easy by comparison. While there had been moments when we'd both been frightened that he might die, they were just that—moments. We'd never had to confront the brutal questions at the heart of Ann and Jim's dialogue: How much more pain could Jim ask Ann to withstand? How much more chemo did Ann have to tolerate to convince her husband and two college-age kids that she was doing everything possible to remain in their lives? At what point could she say, "Enough," without having to worry they might question her love for them?

At least Joe and I didn't have to make decisions about his death. He went seemingly painlessly. He'd once told me that he could never do another transplant and I'd responded, "I could never ask you to do it again." But faced with a little more time with Joe, how gracefully would I have stepped back? I like to think I'd have deferred to his wishes. But how can I know for sure? . . . Death. Choices . . . Who knew I would find gratitude in Joe's slipping away.

It was the start of a heart-wrenching learning curve. Just as Joe and I had taken valuable lessons from his mother's death, I now drew on what I'd learned during Joe's years of illness and in the months since his death to navigate the coming months. Every member of my family had accumulating experience with illness and dying. All of us learned from each other. Ann, the youngest among us, would prove the strongest student and teacher of all.

Ultimately, she withstood four more rounds of chemo. When those failed to have any significant impact on her liver tumors, she halted treatment and told us that from here forward, she intended to focus on the quality of her life. "I wasn't real comfortable with that decision," Jim told me recently. But through the winter and spring, Ann stiffened against suggestions of further treatment, and instead threw herself into maximizing her remaining time. As they had throughout their marriage, Jim and Ann took to the outdoors, hiking, biking, and climbing mountains right up to six weeks before her death. "We had some of the best times of our relationship," Jim recalls. "Looking back, I feel very privileged to have been able to watch her die. I learned a ton from her in terms of the way she helped to prepare me and herself for death."

And Ann learned from her close proximity to Becky and me after Joe's death. During that same trip to Vermont, Jim told me she'd been watching carefully as I made preparations for Joe's burial and memorial service. "Ann has it all under control," he said. After she stopped treatment, Ann took several steps to ease what lay ahead for Jim and their children, Emily and Jeremy. She selected a funeral home, a cemetery, a plot, and a casket; provided a list of candidates to speak at her memorial service; made sure their finances were in order; secured a desirable dorm room for Jeremy for his next year of college.

Telling Jim, "I am expecting you to remarry," Ann drew attention to my relationship with Bob. "We talked about your dating, about your going out and living your life again," Jim told me later. Lifting a page from my mother's playbook, she supplied Jim with the names of single women friends and quietly asked one of them, Patsy, to look after him. At the time I thought her active engagement in her husband's future social life a bit over-the-top. But I changed my mind the day a friend told me about an acquaintance whose final words to his wife had been, "Don't you dare remarry." That self-absorbed dying wish deepened my appreciation for the permission my sister, mother, and husband each gave their spouses to move on with their lives.

Several times during her last months, Ann told me that Becky and I were "role models" for her, Jim, and their kids. Three days after Ann died, I shared that with a Montclair friend who'd lost her parents at a young age. "Look what you gave her," she said approvingly.

"What a horrible thing to give," I said, and burst into tears.

With time, I've come to feel differently. While I have been disinclined to search for meaning in any of the deaths in my life, it's meaningful to me that Ann was able to extract information from the events surrounding Joe's death to help prepare her family for her absence. It's meaningful that after her death, her children felt they could speak openly with me about their grief, and found our talks helpful. And it's meaningful to me that Jim found it "a comfort to know you'd gone through it and dealt with it and were able to move on."

I now understand what my friend Richard meant when, in response to my thanks for sharing his experience, he said, "This was hard-earned. It's a blessing to answer questions and be able to share it." I, too, find solace in the sharing.

I won't detail my sister's and mother's dying months. Neither would want to be remembered that way. (Neither would Joe. Forgive me, Wease, if I've shared too much.) But I know they drew strength from the way our family held together. People outside our immediate circle assumed that each of us was consumed by unremitting sadness and despair, but actually the members of my nuclear six-pack drew considerable comfort from each other.

For me, our sense of togetherness was a gift. I'd felt so achingly alone at times during Joe's illness. How could I not? Our marriage was exclusive, unknowable to anyone but the two of us. My family, by contrast, shared a long, rich history that involved all six of us. Like any family, we'd weathered disappointments and disagreements, bruised feelings and disrupted relationships. Yet, we remained strongly connected. Thanks to parents who'd always encouraged their children to cheer each other's accomplishments and had never fomented envy or competition between us, the sibling bonds were particularly unshakeable—no small feat for four sibs born within five years. Now, all six of us leaned into each other. Never knowing which visit, which conversation, which hug might be the last, each of us was mindful of the others' feelings, communicating messages of love, support, and appreciation aimed at easing distress.

The logistics were horrific. There was my mother down south, frail and withering; there was my sister up north, dealing with multiplying tumors. At precisely the moment we all most needed to be together, the six of us could not arrange to be in the same place at the same time. As Jonathan, Alan, and I ricocheted between Vermont and North Carolina through the first seven months of 2010, it helped tremendously that everyone remained clear-eyed about what lay ahead. All of the sibs, Ann included, hoped that Mom would go first and be spared the devastation of losing her youngest child. But we couldn't count on that. So, my brothers and I quietly fashioned a plan for an Ann-first scenario: Alan would fly up from Florida to be with Mom; Jonathan or I would escort my father to Vermont for Ann's funeral. This was a tremendous sacrifice on Alan's part, one that Jonathan and I let him know we appreciated. When we entered the final days—*Every time the phone rings, I gird, wondering, Is it Ann? Is it Mom? Both are dying quickly*—it enabled us to avoid the sort of confusion and conflict that can rend a family.

Instead, our shared focus on trying to ease Ann's and Mom's physical and emotional discomfort held us together. We were united in supporting their decisions, each of us steering clear of both unsolicited opinions about their medical choices and statements about our own anguish. In hindsight, that unity strikes me as remarkable, particularly given the additional stresses my various family members were shouldering. One month before Ann's death, Esme and I had flown to Oklahoma to finally inter my mother-in-law's ashes.

That was only the start of the burial season. Five days before Ann's death, Jonathan's much-adored mother-in-law died. Five days after Ann's death, my parents lost one of their dearest friends. That same week, Alan's father-in-law was rushed to the hospital, and soon after moved in with Alan's family (where he would remain until his death seven weeks after we buried Mom). Battered by so much death, it would have been understandable if we'd found release in wishful thinking, self-pity, caregiving one-upmanship, pecking-order posturing, even petty squabbles over who would get Mom's silverware—in short, anything that might have distracted from what my friends described as "Too much. So unfair." Yet at no point did any of us lose sight of Ann's or Mom's needs.

Recently, I asked each of my brothers what had helped him most through these months. Jonathan responded, "It was huge that we were united in our thoughts and our desire to help. We were able to put our egos aside and do what they needed, not what we needed." Alan said, "What helped was perspective on life after life. A continuity." That matches up with Bonanno's research, which found that people "with strong beliefs about the afterlife . . . report less worry and fewer anxieties about death." All six members of my family shared such beliefs (though I doubt any of us envisioned the same hereafter). As a result, neither Ann nor my mother feared death; none of those remaining feared letting them move on. "Being okay with death helped us not refuse to let it happen," Jonathan said. "Easing their transition was our job, period."

An abstraction, to be sure, but he's right: it helped us to let go of the departing, as they wished. In the days before Ann's death on August 14 and my mother's less than three weeks later on September 1, there were no disagreements about heroic last measures, no panicked eleventh-hour trips to the hospital, no diverting meltdowns. Ann and Mom each died as they wanted to: quietly, at home, surrounded by people they loved. I take comfort in that.

In the bizarre twilight between their two deaths, my grief couldn't find a place to settle. *I can't fully grieve Ann while Mom is going,* I wrote. After both were gone, my emotional confusion continued. I would start to think about Ann, then think guiltily, *I should be thinking about Mom*—or vice versa. Or I'd think of one of them, and the thought would intrude, *I should be thinking about Wease, too.* I wasn't alone in finding my grief confused by the pile-on of death. Both Alan and Jonathan have told me that eighteen months passed before they began to really feel their grief over the loss of our baby sister. As for me, with Ann's decline following so close on the heels of Joe's death, I was very attuned during her last nine months to my deepening grief about the prospect of losing her, and did most of my crying during that period. It's possible that the most wrenching feelings of loss are behind; it's also possible that my sorrow is on time-delay and may yet catch up with me.

The twelve months that followed my sister's and mother's deaths were marked less by a keen sense of absence, as I experienced after losing Joe, than by a heightened awareness of what was providing solace. Webster's defines solace as "alleviation of grief," and I discovered during these months just how potent a weapon it can be. I didn't choose this coping mechanism; it chose me. Thank God, it did. Absent pockets of comfort, I don't know how I would have tolerated so much sorrow.

It's not that I've forgotten the horror of Ann's and Mom's final months. I well remember the shriveling proportions of my once-fit sister; her bouts of chemo-induced nausea; the sudden, fast drop of her casket into the ground. I remember my mother's hoarse whisper, the tattered remains of the deep voice she used to magical effect on recorded tapes for the blind; the unsettling sight of her pushing back from the dinner table, the food on her plate undisturbed; her body curled up fetal-style after learning of Ann's death. But those sorts of aching memories tend not to arise of their own accord; they usually require summoning.

The memories more likely to surface without bidding are kinder and more gentle. They involve tender words, loving gestures, and small acts of compassion that remind that I did my very best to ease my mother's and sister's suffering, and they did their very best to ease mine. They illustrate how diligently all my family members strove to close the ledger on regrets and to achieve a good good-bye. They underscore how all six of us were guided by the same feeling I articulated in my journal two days before Ann's death: *It feels so important to know that these people I love KNOW that I love them. What else, in the end, can you give but your love?*

A few of those moments:

After Ann halted treatment, she put out word that she had "parted ways with what medicine has to offer," and wanted to spend her remaining months "balancing my work life with things I enjoy doing." Through the winter and spring of 2010, I visited for two- and three-day stretches to help with the cleaning, laundry, and sort of odd jobs that tapped skills Ann swore she didn't know I had. When I ironed one of her work outfits without scorching it, we both laughed in amazement. My ability to mend a fraying quilt drew a shriek of, "Meus! I didn't know you could sew!" (I can't. But, never mind.) It was good for both of us. I needed to feel useful; she increasingly needed help.

Ann also opened her home to friends, and they came in droves. As I moved around her house, I could hear their laughter and snatches of their conversations: "...the impact you've had on my life," "You were the one who convinced me to..." "Do you remember the time we..." One day, I mentioned to Alan how touching it was to hear these tributes. He, in turn, asked if I was planning to write Ann a letter. "A letter?" Yes, he said. He'd written a eulogy that he planned to send her; he wanted her to read it for herself. Was I going to do something similar?

I felt like an idiot. Who knew better than I the quiet joy and consolation of an explicit statement of appreciation? In coming days, each time I returned to Alan's idea, determined to come up with something (I write for a living, for crying out loud), I was unable to traverse time for iconic anecdotes, my mind too crowded by thoughts of Ann's decline and my awareness that while I might someday have another husband, I would never have another sister. Over and over, my brain spewed the same aching refrain: "She's my only sister. She's my only sister."

Finally, it hit me. *That* was the message I wanted to convey to Ann. As soon as I knew the message, I knew the medium, too. From the time we were babies, our mother kept beautiful family scrapbooks, a cut-and-paste hobby that both Ann and I had emulated with our own families. A few months earlier, when my sibs and I had put together a scrapbook for Mom's eightieth birthday, Ann had updated my skills by teaching me how to scan photos into the computer and assemble a digital scrapbook. Now, as I went through my old scrapbooks, hunting for pictures to document my relationship with my sister, I was struck by how much we looked alike. We'd been hearing it for decades, but only now did I really see it. I also began to notice the many mirror-like images. Me with a terrible seventies haircut; Ann with a terrible seventies 'do. Me with Mom at my college graduation; Ann with Mom at hers. Me in my wedding gown, Ann at my side; Ann in her wedding gown, me by hers. There was also ample evidence of our differences, some of them a stitch. My lame idea of athletic derring-do: a handstand. Ann's: a dazzling flight down a zip line.

I wanted to capture all this—us—with photos and words that celebrated our relationship. "Sisters, sisters..." read the opening caption, followed on the next page by, "...there were never such fanfuckingtastic sisters!" I labored for days, struggling to get the nuance of each caption right. Though the words were few and my target audience was just one, I knew this was the most important book I would ever write. I arranged the photos and lighthearted captions to segue from the many shared groupings in our lives—two parents, two (occasionally disgusting) brothers, a deep stash of nieces and nephews—to my message: Ann was singular in my life. Unique. Irreplaceable.

I sat by her side as she unwrapped and read *My One and Only* for the first time. We laughed. We cried. Together, we read the final pages: "You are, Pooz . . . my one and only . . . I will love you forever." Then turning to me, my sister said, with a catch in her voice, "This is the most loving gift I've ever gotten."

I still mist up when I think of her words. It comforts me to know that Ann understood how much I loved her.

In June 2010, Bob and I embarked on what we dubbed the Moms Tour. This little adventure was way premature. We'd been together only five months. Each of us was widowed barely a year; neither of us was anywhere near ready to think about the sort of permanent commitment that we knew was on our aging mothers' minds. But these were two very determined Jewish mamas, their stereophonic chorus of "I want to meet him/her" growing more insistent with each passing month. It felt a bit ridiculous—Bob, sixty-one, and me, fifty-five, setting off to obtain each mother's "blessing"—but we understood they wanted reassurance that their bereaved children had a happy future in store. We aimed to put their minds at ease.

Over a whirlwind weekend, we flew first to Florida to visit Bob's eighty-eight-year-old widowed mother. We weren't in Tampa more than a few hours before Mariam got down to business: "I don't understand why the two of you aren't getting married." Repeatedly she said that she was counting down the days and felt very ready to die—but not before she could rest easy that her Robert would be taken care of. Endearingly old-world, she fussed, she fed, she tried to tease out promises that when Robert returned from work each day (Bob: "Mom, Jill works, too"), he would find a clean home and a cooked supper (Me: "Um, I don't like to cook, but Bob does"). It was kind of comical, but I knew what Mariam was looking for. I gave her assurances of my love for Bob; she gave me recipes.

We flew next to North Carolina. Typically, I visit my parents one to two times a year; in recent years each of those visits had been dominated by my mother's talk of death. During my last visit, Mom had been so focused on her desire to die, I on my grief over losing Joe, that we'd talked right past each other. We'd each been left feeling the other didn't understand. While I had confidence that we would approach this visit with the same mutual determination to do "our best by each other" that I'd noted a year earlier in my letter to her, I didn't expect to encounter the energetic, upbeat woman she once had been.

Mom astonished me. She was engaging and engaged, a delightful hostess and a delighted mother. She revived her humor, her formidable storytelling skills, her hard-to-resist charm. She offered her unqualified approval of Bob, not by talking about marriage (which she knew I would hate), but by radiating joy in my newfound happiness. I felt like I had my mother back, the one whose vitality and confidence—in herself, in me, in the future—had been such a source of strength through most of my life. I was ebullient. So was Dad. "I haven't seen her this well in years," he told me.

That visit, undertaken to convince my mother she could stop worrying about me, proved a huge gift—for me. In addition to seeing my mother's energy revive, I saw the strong connection between my parents rekindle. Though their mutual devotion had never flagged, the spark between them had dimmed beneath the weight of my mother's illness and its demands on my father's time. Now, as I watched them relax back into the pleasure they took in one another's company, I was reminded what an incredible couple they were.

Months later at my mother's memorial service, unexpectedly called upon to speak, I fell back on that old standby: things my mother taught me. The list was familiar until I heard myself say, "My mother taught me the joy of relationships. Were it not for the example of my parents, the joy they took in one another, I don't think I could have opened myself so soon to new love." The thought hadn't occurred to me until that moment. But as soon as I said it, I knew it was true. If I have any regret now that my mother is gone, it's that I didn't articulate that idea to myself in time to share it with her. We'd both worked so hard during her final months to achieve a fitting good-bye. That sentiment would have been a perfect coda to Bob's and my visit.

Instead, it was my mother who offered the perfect message as we parted, one that cut to the core of her strongest beliefs, leaving no doubt how she felt in her deepest heart about our often rocky relationship. "I must have done something very right," she said, "to have you as my daughter in this incarnation." (Okay. I'm crying.)

Five weeks before Ann's death, my family convened in Vermont for the Prouty, an annual cancer-research fundraiser sponsored by the

Dartmouth-Hitchcock Medical Center, where Ann had undergone surgery and received treatment. A year earlier, Ann had spearheaded a team of bikers and hikers who'd raised more research dollars than any other team. She was determined to do it again. In a candid letter designed to woo donors and new teammates, she described the course of her cancer, her decision months earlier to abandon treatment and focus on "quality of life," her doctors' prognosis that she had "months, not years" remaining. "So, for me, participating in the Prouty is quite personal," she wrote. "I share this with you not because I want your sympathy. I don't. Rather, I hope you'll join me in this meaningful, fun and inspiring event that does much to advance research in finding cures for cancer."

To no one's surprise, she fielded another winning team. Everyone—teammates, friends, colleagues, strangers—cheered wildly as Ann stepped up to the podium to claim her team's prize. My father, my brothers, and I, shrieked, "Go, Pooz!"

We could have cared less about the damn fundraiser.

Back in April when Ann had sent out her letter, she'd signaled she wanted all of us to participate. My mother's health needs had kept my father from visiting either me during Joe's illness or Ann after her surgery; Dad was hell-bent on being on hand for this. So was my brother Alan, who, in addition to being my father's main caregiving backup, had for years been dealing with parent-in-law health issues that required he remain in Florida. After Dad secured a professional caregiver for my mother, Alan booked tickets for himself, his wife, and his son. That prompted Jonathan to invite his three kids. Except for my mother and Becky (who was again off at camp), this was shaping up to be the first full-blown family gathering in years. Knowing that Alan wanted to meet the new man in my life, I said to Bob, "You come, too."

While there had never been much doubt this would be the last time we would gather around Ann as a family, I hadn't anticipated—I don't think any of us had—how quickly she would fade. When she invited us in April, she was in hiking-swimming-working mode. By the time the Prouty rolled around in early July, she was dropping weight, feeling exhausted, and relying on pain medication. My family was gathering to say good-bye. Bob didn't belong there.

As the weekend approached, I felt my resistance building. I didn't want Bob to come to Vermont, but I didn't know how to say this to him. Instead, I said I would be focused on my family and was concerned he might feel bored and left out. Bob swatted that away. He could entertain himself. He just wanted to be there for me. "Don't give it another thought," he said.

But I did, and as we drove north that weekend, I stewed about my mistake.

I couldn't have been more wrong. It pretty much says everything you need to know about my family at that moment in time that Bob and I, each widowed barely a year and still grieving our spouses, provided the one ray of sunshine at this cloud-covered gathering. I could feel the eyes on us and see the smiles every time Bob and I touched. Each of my sibs pulled me aside to say how happy they were to see me in such an affectionate relationship. Ann's daughter, Emily, coaxed me behind the garage to sneak cigarettes and dish about boyfriends. My other niece and my nephews were eager to hear the details of how we'd met. Both Jim and my father, pressed repeatedly by their wives to look for new mates quickly, told me that at some point up the road they'd like to learn more about online dating. Over and over, people said they loved that Bob and I had found each other.

Of course they did. We were the hope, the promise, the proof that life goes on.

As for Bob, he did just as he promised: he left me free to move about while he took care of himself. Several times I spotted him conversing with one family member or another, but his efforts didn't penetrate until I later heard from them, one after another, how much they'd enjoyed getting to know him. What did come through during our Vermont stay was how much time Bob was spending with Jim on the porch, drinking beer and chatting as they manned the grill. I suspect that just as I made use of my behind-the-shed chats with Emily to talk a bit about preparing for death and dealing with grief, Bob used some of that time with Jim to do the same.

Bob's and my experience—our willingness to venture forward six months after our spouses' deaths, our irrepressible delight in one another despite our grief, our families' warm embrace of our relationship—made an impression. Six months after Ann's death, Jim formed an attachment with Patsy, the Dartmouth classmate and colleague Ann had asked to look out for him. Six months after Mom's death, Dad formed an attachment with a woman in his retirement village. I'd been so uncertain about the appropriateness of dating so soon after Joe died. It consoles me that Bob and I, by example, provided a sort of permission that helped my father and Jim begin rebuilding their lives quickly—just as my mother and sister had wanted.

When I returned to Vermont two weeks after the Prouty gathering, the deterioration in Ann's condition was dramatic. Bed-ridden and in constant pain, she was declining visitors, except for family, which at this point meant Jonathan, Gatha, and me. Yet Ann was determined to tell her boss, in person, that she couldn't work any longer. I drove Ann to the Dartmouth campus and, holding her arm, helped her up the steps of an ivy-covered building. When Ann spotted her boss at the top of the center staircase, she shook me off.

I have no idea where she found the strength to climb those steps, let alone the strength to remain upright through that hour-long meeting. When it ended, Ann returned to bed, where she would remain for the rest of my visit.

The next day, too weak to sit up, she dictated letters to me. These were Prouty thank-you notes, but each was also a farewell. Ann was teary, her voice choked with emotion as she struggled to find the right words. At one point the phone rang and a friend asked to speak with her. Ann shook her head and mouthed, "No." After I hung up, she said, "We already said good-bye. I can't do it again. It hurts too much."

When I'd witnessed my sister and father's final embrace at the end of the Prouty weekend, I'd been focused on Dad's face, his expression of agony as he said good-bye—forever—to his youngest child. Only now did it occur to me how painful it must be for Ann to go through parting after parting with the people she loved.

So when Ann told me as we hugged good-bye that this would be our last visit, I didn't push back or question her. "I understand," I said. After I drove away from her house, I pulled off to the side of the road and wept. When I got home, I phoned Lynn, who like me is the older of two sisters. I knew she would appreciate the depth of my anguish. Instead, when I said I'd just seen Ann for the last time, she offered a response that startled me: "How do you know that?"

"Because every good-bye takes too much out of Ann. She doesn't want any more visitors."

"But you're her *sister*," Lynn said, her tone appalled. "She doesn't mean you."

"Yes, she *does* mean me," I responded emphatically. "This isn't about me or what I want. It's about Ann and what *she* wants."

Ann would live two and a half more weeks. Every one of those days, it was painful for me to remain at the remove she'd requested.

I found solace then—and I still take comfort now—in knowing that I stepped aside from that pain to give Ann what she needed. This was a lesson different from the one my mother had taught me about the importance of reassuring a loved one that you will be okay if they move on. *It's not just about giving a loved one permission to let go,* I wrote after my conversation with Lynn. *It is hearing them when they tell you they need you to let go.*

On August 13, I flew to North Carolina to be with my parents. My father sounded so exhausted on the phone; I wanted to provide some backup support. *Stunned by just how yellow Mom is. Mustard colored. Not just her skin, but her eyes, too.* For years, my mother had been offering Ann and me her beautiful diamond engagement ring; for years we'd each been hoping the other would take it. Ann, a nail biter, had never liked to wear rings; I, with my big knuckles that swell in humid weather, had long since sworn off all but my wedding band. And neither of us was inclined to sport a large diamond.

But this time, when my mother offered her ring, I said, "Yes, I'd love to have it." Though I knew I wouldn't wear it often, I meant it. My mother had designed this ring and worn it throughout my life. I felt it belonged with one of her daughters. Clearly, Ann wasn't going to take it. My mother looked so pleased as I slipped the ring onto the fourth finger of my right hand. A perfect fit. "I'll think of you every time I wear it," I said.

I meant that, too. Whenever I put on a piece of gifted jewelry, I think of the person who gave it to me. Since Joe's death, I'd made it (and continue to make it) a point to wear a piece of his jewelry every day. During my final visit with Ann, she'd insisted that I take any of her jewelry that I liked, particularly her earrings, a mutual fetish of longstanding. Each day since then, I'd been wearing her earrings, some of them pairs I'd given her.

That evening as my father and I dressed to go to the retirement village dining room, I saw Mom mouth to Dad, "She's wearing the ring." It gave me such pleasure to know she was pleased. After dinner, I walked Dad to his car, then set out on foot for my parents' house, planning to call Bob while I walked. As I dug my cell phone from my purse, I suddenly felt the weight of it all: *Joe's necklace, Ann's earrings, Mom's ring. It all felt so very heavy. Literally. My gait slowed.* I had to sit. I had to cry. The trip back took longer than I'd anticipated.

When I rejoined my parents, I found them in the living room watching a televised tennis match. Around 9:00, the phone rang. It was Jim. Ann was gone.

During the next confused hour, I was too torn in two directions to register my own reaction. It was so clear that each of my parents needed the other, but each was too upset to offer the other comfort. Instead, my father went to his computer and began trawling the Internet for flights to Vermont; my mother went to their bed, curled herself in a ball, and cried. I first sat with my mother. When my father began fuming loudly that he couldn't make his computer work, I went to his office to help. Back and forth, back and forth. At one point, my father walked into the bedroom, said "How are you, sweetheart?" to my mother, then promptly went back to his office. That was when my mother started to sob. I could see she needed him to put his arms around her; I could see he needed to keep moving. So, I did something I don't recall ever doing before: I lay down behind my mother, spooned her body with mine, and wrapped my arms around her. She took hold of my hand. And there we lay, alone, together in our sorrow.

The next day, as my brothers and I had planned, Alan drove from Florida to be with my mother; I escorted my father to

Vermont. What I hadn't anticipated was how wrong everything would feel the next day when we approached the open grave in the mountainside cemetery that Ann had selected. It wasn't only that my family was burying its youngest member; it was that we weren't all together to do this hideous task. Impulsively, I pulled my cell phone from my purse, dialed Alan, and said, "Would you and Mom like me to leave this cell open so you can hear the service?" There were murmurs, then Alan said, "Yes."

I didn't think of them again as the funeral unfolded. There were too many other painful emotions crowding my mind. *My sister, oh God, my sister.* And then, there was my father. In the months leading up to Ann's death, Dad had said repeatedly, "This isn't the natural order of things. A parent shouldn't have to bury his child." It's one thing to consider that idea as an abstraction; it's another to stand graveside, your fingers laced with your father's, watching your sister—your father's baby—lowered into the ground. When the coffin suddenly dropped so quickly that we expelled a collective gasp, I felt Dad teeter. Tightening my grip, I didn't ease up until I felt him regain his balance. To his left, Jonathan grabbed Gatha, whose knees had buckled.

Dad was steady when, in accordance with Jewish tradition, he stepped forward to shovel dirt onto the casket. One by one, we followed. When my turn came, I bypassed the shovel. While burying Joe, I'd wanted to feel the dirt, maybe to drive home the finality of it all. As with Joe, so with Ann: I grabbed a handful of dirt with my right hand and released it into the grave.

A few minutes later, as I gathered up my cell phone and walked back to the car, my thoughts returned to my mother. Suddenly, I thought of something that might give her comfort. "Alan," I said into the phone, "tell Mom that when I threw the dirt on Ann's coffin, I did it with the hand that has her engagement ring on it. She was there, too." Instead, Alan put my mother on the line. "I was wearing your ring when I threw the dirt onto Ann's coffin," I repeated. "I want you to know your hand touched the soil, too."

Two days later, my father called me in New Jersey to tell me that my mother wasn't doing well, but wanted to talk with me. When she came on the line, she was breathless, her words coming in short bursts. "That was a wonderful thing you did for me, wearing the ring and then throwing the dirt," she said. "I appreciate that." Our conversation wandered off to discuss a visit she'd had with two of her brothers. Then she cut off my questions. "That's not why I'm calling," she said. "I'm calling about you."

"I love you," I said. "You know that, right?"

"I know that. Okay. Bye."

My mother would linger seventeen more days, alternately weeping and sleeping as her skin tone turned from yellow to what Alan described as a macabre shade of orange. Though I'm certain Mom and I spoke again, I don't remember those conversations. Nor do I remember the call—Alan? Dad?—informing me that she had passed on. By default or by unconscious design, my last active memory of my mother is the conversation we had two days after Ann's burial. That she and I, after so many years of trying and failing each other, had finally gotten it right—well, it helps.

12

COMMEMORATION

As with death and dying, so with burial and commemoration: this was a learning process, each new experience enlarging my understanding of the ways we say good-bye and how those farewells inform our grief. Prior to the deaths in my family, I'd attended only a handful of funerals, all of which adhered to religious prescription. My experience with memorial services ran a wider range. I'd been to somber gatherings held directly before burial, where the bereaved family entered in black and leaned on one another as they walked down the center aisle to their seats; I'd been to boozy "celebrations" weeks or months after a death, where people sprawled on lawns or dined under tents and danced late into the night. Cumulatively, these experiences had left me with a sense that funerals were for driving home the message that the deceased was irretrievably gone; commemoration services were for stirring and reinforcing happier memories that would help those who remained behind to hold the departed in their hearts and minds.

With Joe, I had only a broad sense of the sort of memorial service he wanted, and no guidance about his burial. I wanted both events to honor Wease in a manner I thought he'd have felt fitting, but I didn't want either event to lend needlessly to Becky's upset or mine. Lingering memories from a few of those earlier post-death gatherings helped steer my choices.

One involved a young *Newsweek* colleague who'd died suddenly while swimming laps during a workday lunch. Adhering to Jewish tradition, Kirk's stunned family scheduled a memorial service immediately after his death, and Joe and I attended, along with everyone else in our department. While the eulogies left no particular impression, one of the widow's choices did. She, too, had written a eulogy, but had someone else read it. As I'd never met the woman, I could only surmise that she either dreaded falling apart before the large crowd or didn't want to subject herself to scrutinizing eyes. Whatever her reason, I thought her choice very sane. Generous, too. Who, after all, could speak more intimately about Kirk than she?

At the end of the service, congregants were invited to accompany the family to the cemetery. When our editor indicated he was going, we all dutifully followed. As I stood on the fringes of the assemblage, holding Joe's hand, I remember thinking, *We don't belong here.* To my mind, the gaping hole in the ground, the tears, the mournful liturgy demanded the intimacy of family. Joe and I were little better than gawkers. Joe told me he felt the same way.

Two decades later, Joe and I attended another memorial service, this one for a *People* colleague neither of us had known well. Held many weeks after Jim's death, the church service had a coherence that left me with the impression that his widow had given a lot of thought to what she wanted people to take from the day. As each speaker described not only Jim's strengths and triumphs, but also his weaknesses and battles, a three-dimensional picture emerged. By the time I exited the church, I knew Jim far better than I had when I first slid into a rear pew. On the drive home, Joe and I wondered if Jim would have welcomed this send-off, but we agreed that the eulogies had seared him in our minds more vividly than a series of fond reminiscences.

Finally, there were the burial arrangements for Joe's parents, who had been precise about their wishes. Al wanted his cremated remains scattered off the coast of Chicago, his childhood home-town; Short wanted hers interred in her family cemetery in Pryor, Oklahoma. This made no sense to either Joe and me or Esme and her husband, Robert. Why would a couple devoted to each other for so many decades not want to be laid to rest side by side? At several Christmas gatherings we'd pressed them to reconsider. But, no, that was what each of them wanted.

So after Al died in June 2005, Joe and I met up with Esme and Robert in Chicago, rented a boat, chugged out into the roiling waters of Lake Michigan, and scattered Al's ashes. Though we laughed when the lake wind blew the ashes back in our faces, and achieved some intimacy as Joe and Esme told Pop stories, it felt wrong to all of us that Short, too frail for a motorboat outing, was not on hand to bury her husband of sixty-three years. It also felt wrong that Short's remains would not eventually join Al's in this place.

What I took from that day proved to be something quite differ-ent. Al had been a quiet man, routinely upstaged by his gregarious, opinionated wife. The day of his burial at sea, Al had the spotlight all to himself. "It reminds me of that line in *Death of a Salesman*, 'Attention must be paid,'" I said to Joe. "Maybe that was what your father had in mind all along."

Maybe it was what Short had in mind, too, but I doubt that her burial resembled what she'd imagined. After Short's death in March 2009, Esme stashed the urn containing her mother's ashes on the top shelf of her laundry room. The plan was for the same crew of children and children-in-law to trek to Pryor to inter those remains. But, Joe got sick. Then, Joe died. Then, Robert developed foot problems. Not wanting Esme to bury Short alone, I promised I would accompany her to Pryor. But then my sister and mother went into decline. As the months ticked past the first anniversary of Short's death, Esme told me, with a weak laugh, that we better get to Oklahoma soon. That urn was creeping the hell out of her cleaning woman.

One month before Ann's death, Esme and I finally converged in a Texas airport and flew together to Oklahoma. Hoping to forge a sense of connection to the place, we drove to Short's family homestead, which had long since passed from family hands, and toured the house with the current owner. At the cemetery, while Esme studied generations of family headstones, I tried to summon memories of Short, but thoughts of Ann, Mom, and Joe kept intruding. Short had lived a long, productive life. She'd already been gone fifteen months. The best Esme and I could muster was a dry-eyed, "Pax requiem, Short." Attention had been paid, but it felt so inadequate.

As we drove away, it occurred to me that neither Esme nor I would likely ever return to this place, and a sense of melancholy settled over me. I felt sad that anyone who read Short's headstone in the future was likely to be a stranger. And I felt sad for Esme that should she desire to visit her parents' graves, she was unlikely to find satisfaction. One was buried at a distant remove; the other was scattered in a distant lake.

The elder Treens were on my mind the day I selected Joe's burial site. While I knew I was unlikely to pay graveside visits, I couldn't know what Becky's inclination might be. When I found a spot that I hoped would summon happy memories for her as well as sad ones, I purchased the adjacent plot, too, feeling that whatever turns my life might take, Becky shouldn't have to hopscotch around the country if she wanted to visit her parents' graves. I also aimed to make my eventual burial as hassle-free for her as possible. Should I remarry, I didn't want Becky to have to choose which man I should be buried beside. This would be a clear statement: Dad and Mom—Forever. Given Joe's bewildered reaction to his parents' choices, I'm certain he would have wanted this for our child.

The funeral service was also in keeping with the man I knew: intimate and loving; free of religious officiants and texts that held no place in our lives; confined to a tight circle of loved ones that insured against the sort of gawking that had made both of us uncomfortable at Kirk's burial. The crowd numbered only seven: Esme and Robert, Jonathan and Ann, Becky and me, and Becky's former babysitter, Gay, whom I could count on to comfort Becky at a moment when I doubted I would be able to. I'd asked Robert, Esme, and Jonathan each to "say something," and I remember that I was deeply moved by each of their brief eulogies.

Yet little of our time spent graveside left a deep impression. Maybe it was the smallness of the plot. The generic quality of the silver urn. The lateness of the day, precisely one month after Joe's death. (The autopsy had held up the burial for two weeks; Becky's camping trip had held it up two weeks more.) By the time we put Joe's ashes in the ground, my feeling was less numb shock than a resigned need to get through this grim task. That, and an intense feeling of aloneness. Though my daughter, siblings, and in-laws were on hand, the person I most needed beside me at this I-can't-handle-this-alone moment was the man who had been beside me through all the I-can't-handle-this-alone moments of the last twenty-seven years. But he was the one going into the ground. So, I stood there handling the unhandleable, feeling very alone.

After the brief, improvised ceremony, I stayed behind to release a few more handfuls of dirt into the grave. I whispered words of love. But as I'd felt when I kissed Joe before the EMTs carried him out of our country kitchen, this felt more theatrical than real. In my head, I'd been talking to Wease constantly since his death. Any one of those interior monologues—in bed, on the commuter bus, even in the bathroom—felt more connected to Joe than directing my thoughts toward an urn in the ground.

In the three years since then, neither Becky nor I have felt drawn to the cemetery, though it's only minutes from our house. Each year on the anniversary of Joe's death, we make it a point to visit his grave together and let the conversation wander where it may. On none of our visits has Becky asked to bring flowers to perch against the upright headstone (um, monument), and I haven't initiated the gesture. The idea of placing flowers on Joe's grave does nothing for me. The idea that his ashes are just inches from the soles of my shoes does nothing for me either.

Only once has Joe's burial place stirred strong emotion in me. Three months after his interment, I returned to the cemetery with Ann to inspect the headstone, newly installed beside Joe's grave. The simple inscription— Joseph M. Treen 1942–2009—sliced me like a newly sharpened knife. "He's very dead," I murmured to my sister. Then, I burst into tears.

Joe's memorial service, by contrast, made him both painfully and wonderfully alive to me. As promised, Ken and Arthur hosted the event at their house, but thanks to Lynn's quiet intervention, more than venue and menu considerations were lifted from my shoulders. "I didn't know your grief," Lynn would tell me later, "but I knew *you*. I knew the Martha Stewart-ish jobs were going to stress you out." She, Becky's godfathers, and two other Pennsylvania friends, Paige and Phil, handled not only the catering, but the tent, chairs, speaker system, flowers, drinks, and booze (then, despite my efforts to reimburse them, most of the tab, as well).

My own to-do list was short: invite the guests, line up the

speakers, order the programs. The invitation part was easy. Using the Weasel Update e-mail list, I extended an invitation to anyone who wanted to come. If someone cared enough about Joe, Becky, or me to want to attend, I wanted them there. Ken and Arthur had plenty of room. Lining up speakers was easy, too. Joe's best friend from college, who'd been the best man at our wedding, said he would be honored to officiate. Every person I asked to participate in the service expressed a similar sentiment. That left me to fuss over the program and introductions for each of the speakers. But writing is my comfort zone; thanks to my friends, I never had to leave it.

The morning after Joe's funeral, Ken and Arthur's house filled with our Pennsylvania friends to help with preparations for the 4:30 p.m. memorial service. "It felt like a barn-raising," Lynn told me. "Everyone who loved you would have given their right arm to help you."

Two hundred people turned out for our "Celebration of Joe." Despite the large crowd, there was a feeling of intimacy beneath the white tent, heightened by a gentle rain that fell throughout the service, providing a soothing audio backdrop to the eulogies delivered from the "dais," Joe's old stand-up typewriter stand. Afterwards, when we headed indoors for the reception, a digital photo show assembled by Esme flashed images of Joe on the downstairs walls; upstairs, my nephew Alex, who'd filmed the service, invited guests to sit before a video camera and offer their own reminiscences. The subject was Joe. The star was Joe. The spirit of the day was Joe.

Here, in other words, was Joe's dream party, the one he would have loved us to throw had I not been such a reluctant hostess. Only this affair was better than his fantasies could have conjured or his modesty would have allowed. Because the setting was Ken and Arthur's elegant home, and because they had overseen every detail, it was far lovelier than Joe and I ever could have managed.

More amazing, pretty much everyone Joe cared about was there. As friends, many of whom Joe hadn't seen in years, arrived from all parts of the country, a patter began in my head: *Where are you, Wease? You should be seeing this.*

During the service, that changed to, *Where are you, Wease? You should be hearing this.* With each new eulogy, the refrain grew louder. It felt so wrong that Joe wasn't hearing these tributes. The ten speakers, most of them fellow journalists, not only had dug deep to tap their fondest memories of Joe, but they'd crafted their remarks beautifully. Evocative, humorous, and moving, each eulogy built upon the one that had come before, in aggregate summoning a clear image of an amazing man—*my* man. I felt so proud of Joe as I sat between Ann and Becky, laughing, crying and, to my surprise, learning something new about my husband.

I'd arranged the speakers chronologically to follow Joe's life from high school through college, on into his journalism career, then forward into marriage and parenthood. I'd given each speaker the same brief spiel: "You represent [whatever] period in Joe's life. I'm hoping this service will be more celebratory than somber. And please, no more than five minutes." I'd offered no suggestions or requests, so I had no idea what any of them would say. Neither did they, since most them didn't know each other. Yet the portrait of Joe that emerged was so consistent it almost sounded scripted: his youthful spirit, his writing talent, his charm, his unflaunted good looks, his lack of pretension, his modesty, his devilish humor, his devotion to Becky and me.

What caught me by surprise was another thread that wove through the eulogies with such persistence that it came to glitter brightest. It began with the first speaker, a high school buddy, who said, "Joe was always there for me." Next, a college friend spoke of how Joe was "unfailingly kind and helpful when we were struggling with school papers." A *People* colleague described Joe as "my go-to guy, as he was for so many friends. If any friend was looking for work or hoping to hire, if your child needed an internship . . . Joe was always there with real help and solid counsel." Speaking for the Pennsylvania contingent, Arthur eulogized, "Joe's expression always seemed to reflect a generous spirit. 'Maybe I can help?'" On behalf of the Smolowe clan (yes, Wease, just one), Jonathan spoke of how Joe "helped people in need, and without fanfare," then described how during his last hospitalization he'd helped our nephew Jeremy pursue an eBay scam artist after the guy made off with two thousand of Jeremy's hard-earned dollars. A *Newsweek* colleague even offered a word to describe Joe's special brand of helpfulness. "If you were his friend," he said, "Joe was your encourager." An encourager, he explained, was someone who helps others realize their dreams.

All of this bespoke a generosity of spirit that was essential to, even defining of, the man Joe had been. Yet while I, too, had benefited from Joe's encouragement, it wouldn't have occurred to me to list "generous" among his most outstanding qualities. Only rarely, I now grasped, had he told me about his efforts on other people's behalf. I doubt that Joe had been purposefully withholding; I think, rather, that it hadn't occurred to him to recount his deeds. Too modest to boast, too self-deprecating to see himself in shining armor, he'd simply acted. Joe, I'm convinced, would have been very surprised and deeply moved to learn that so many people remembered him, above all, as helpful and generous.

Damn it, Wease, where are you? You should be hearing this!

As for my own eulogy, it contained nothing Wease hadn't heard before. But with Joe, I'd had more than a quarter century to express my love and appreciation. Now, I had just five minutes. I honed and honed that damn thing, reluctantly leaving memories on the cutting floor as I settled on the handful of anecdotes that would illustrate Joe's character, talents, playfulness, humor, and, above all, love as both a father and a husband. Inspired by our colleague Jim's memorial service, I tried to capture Joe's and my marriage as it truly had been: not a perfect union, but a unique and dynamic one that despite, or because of, our differences remained animated and engaging to the very end.

I strove for the lightness and humor befitting a "celebration" of Joe. But the idea I most wanted to convey was this: "Not once in all our years together did I ever find Wease boring . . . During the six-month period that he and I spent most of our days alone together in hospital rooms, he made me feel appreciated and so very loved. Even on those days when Wease was too weak to get out of bed, we found pleasure in our conversation. We continued to discuss. Debate. Reassure. Commiserate. Joke. Call each other out on our respective bullshit. Shore each other up. Express our admiration and love. Throughout our twenty-seven years together, the conversation between us never faltered."

Later, several people told me they found that remarkable. During my time with Wease, so did I.

I still do.

Given the occasion, I knew there was no way I could voice such sentiments without bursting into sobs. So, emulating Kirk's wife, I asked my sister to read my eulogy for me. Restored to full Poozian mode by her "miracle patient" status (its unraveling still three months away), Ann launched into a typically animated performance. Only when she began to fight tears midway through did it occur to me how inconsiderate my request had been. She loved Joe. She loved Joe and me as a couple. How blind of me not to anticipate that this would be hard on her, too.

Looking back, I am even more appalled by my thoughtlessness.

Ann was battling cancer, for God's sake. Beneath her flowy outfit that day she was wearing portable chemo apparatus; ahead lay the liver resection surgery (later cancelled) that she dreaded. And her optimism was fading. Two weeks earlier she'd told me, "My cancer symptoms are back." With Joe not yet in the ground, Ann's unsettling news found a place in my journal, but not in my memory. Instead, the Ann who emerges from the foggy month between Joe's death and his burial is a sister who selflessly focused on my needs and lifted me with her energy.

In my daze, I hadn't grasped how closely Ann was watching and learning from my experience. Before her death, she handed her husband a memo that ran slightly more than a single-spaced page. Titled "Thoughts about burial, celebration, finding closure," it included a list of options for her burial, complete with prices. The opening reads: "I really like how Jill handled Joe's burial and service. Similarly, I think that having a private burial and some kind of celebration afterwards may be helpful to you and the kids in terms of closure. My wishes are solely based on what feels right to you." She offered Jim suggestions for memorial speakers, some of the names asterisked. "These are people who I think the kids might resonate to. I know that Becky had a favorite speaker and his words meant the most to her. I think it's important to consider who you and the kids want to hear from."

So, Ann had absorbed the uplifting effect the eulogies were having on Becky and me as she held my hand through Joe's memorial service, the two of us turning often to each other to share our tears and laughter. Had Ann also absorbed the many expressions of regret that day about cancelled lunches, missed phone calls, and postponed get-togethers? Had she banked the comment I whispered in her ear, "Joe should be here to hear this"?

I think she did. Five months later when it became clear that medicine could offer no more miracles, Ann opened her home, giving the people she loved a chance to make the lunch date, place the phone call, schedule the visit. They arrived bearing gifts of fresh-baked pastries, blankets, homemade books, and self-mixed CDs.

But the greatest gift was the one Ann gave each of them: the opportunity to say good-bye.

After the emotional distancing that time had afforded too plentifully in the case of my mother-in-law's burial, and to a lesser extent Joe's, I was unprepared for the raw shock that attends a swift funeral. Ann had told Jim that she should be laid out in a simple pine casket and interred quickly, a Jewish custom that honored my parents. Everyone in the family was reeling as we approached the mountainside grave less than forty-eight hours after her death. Having placed Joe's and Short's small urns in shallow holes, I wasn't prepared for the enormity of the rectangular opening in the ground. Nor was I prepared for the effort required to maneuver Ann's casket along the pitched slope from the hearse to the grave. Gatha, close to eighty, insisted on helping the men and looked like she might topple.

After we fanned out in a loose circle, Jim, his kids and brother on one side, Dad, Jonathan, Gatha, and me on the other, Jim explained that in his Mennonite faith, the funeral tradition was for people to speak if they felt so moved. I hadn't known this was coming, and as Jonathan offered his beautiful prepared remarks, followed by Dad, who spoke movingly of his love for Ann and his pride in her accomplishments, I felt increasingly at a loss. For Joe, my eulogy had been honed over a period of weeks. Now as I stared at Ann's coffin, my mind went blank. We had a lifetime—a *lifetime*—of experiences together. Yet I could think of nothing to say.

No surprise, that. During Ann's last month I'd become aware of my paucity of memories after Alan e-mailed me the eulogy he intended to send her. Alan's adoring stories, which captured our baby sister's infectious enthusiasm, brash fearlessness, and inexhaustible generosity, had managed to jar loose one of my own memories, a moment that I hadn't thought of in decades. But it was small and inconsequential and in no way spoke to Ann's essence.

Now as we stood graveside, I saw Dad's head turn and felt his eyes on me. I had to—I *wanted* to—pay tribute to my one and only sister. I saw no other option. "I don't know why this moment sticks with me," I said, "but it's been playing over and over in my head."

We're young, maybe ten and seven, seated on the wood floor of the yellow-painted bedroom that we'd once shared and now is Ann's alone. As we play a game of jacks, we also try to memorize the lyrics of "America" on Simon & Garfunkel's *Bookends* album. Back and forth we pass the red ball, round after round of jacks. Every time the song ends, I move the record player needle back to the beginning of the "America" track until we've both mastered all the verses.

That's it. Just us. The jacks. The song. It felt so inadequate. No tribute at all.

Back home the following night, I held an impromptu gathering in honor of Ann, cohosted by her Dartmouth classmate Priscilla, with whom I'd cofounded the Montclair Writers Group. During Joe's shiva, almost all the women in our group had met Ann. Now, alongside the cheese and crackers, I set out my copy of *My One and Only*, and my friends paid it the due they knew I needed. Maybe because they were so generous with their praise, I told them about my dismal performance at graveside. Out of a lifetime of memories, I'd managed to come up with just one tiny moment, one that said nothing about the remarkable woman Ann had been, one that failed to pay tribute to her many accomplishments, one that . . .

oh, hell, I couldn't even say why *that* one. "Just two sisters," I said, "enjoying each other, without agenda."

Well. First they Googled and dated the release of S&G's *Bookends* album. 1968. So, Ann and I were more like thirteen and ten, a far greater maturity gap than ten and seven. Then, coming to my rescue with their intelligence and kindness, these wonderful women deconstructed the hell out of my little jacks story. A few snippets:

Eileen: "Home. Play. Safety. Music. This is 'America' as we iconically envision it, yet seemingly rarely is home life so tranquil, safe, and loving."

Priscilla: "Sisters are frustrated with each other all the time. There was none of that in this moment. I love the traveling part in the song. You're both travelers."

Nora: "That song is about love. I love this story."

Marla: "You're like girlfriends, not sisters. You're on the teen side; she's still fairly young. It shouldn't necessarily have worked."

Kim: "It suggests a depth of connection. Many girls who are thirteen would rather die than go back in age to playing jacks. And you let her into your world by sharing the song."

Lynn: "You showed Ann how to die, with Joe. That song, about teenage sexuality, was also seeing the world through your eyes."

Gwen: "I thought, Dang! You had someone to play jacks with you! It was one of the small moments with your sister. Isn't that what life is all about?"

How could I not love that tiny memory (how could I not love these supportive friends) after that? They burnished the moment into something that glistened with meaning. They helped me to see it was not only a fitting tribute, but a perfect one. Not to Ann—but to our irreplaceable bond as sisters.

Eighteen days after we buried Ann, my family congregated again, this time in North Carolina to bury my mother. Though this burial was also swift, we were all steadier this go-round, our sorrow unattended by the devastation that had overwhelmed us at Ann's grave site. We were all grateful my mother was no longer in physical pain. And burying someone who is eighty feels very different than burying someone who is fifty-one. My mother's time had come. We understood this to be the natural order of things. As family members spoke at the small funeral Mom had requested, I could hear each of us starting to push through the cloud that had overhung my mother's last five years to retrieve the woman who, for decades, had been the sun around which we all revolved.

My mother didn't want an obituary, nor did she want her aging friends summoned from afar for a memorial service. Just do something simple that will satisfy our retirement village friends' need to gather, she'd told my father. To me, this felt right. Until her final years, my mother had starred every day on a stage that was uniquely her own. As an actress and a lecturer, she'd enjoyed countless ovations. She felt no need for posthumous applause or reviews. Death, in her view, was a new beginning, not an ending. She was planning to move on.

She was counting on all of us to do the same.

By the time of Ann's memorial service, eight days after my mother's funeral, I was emotionally wrung out. As I made the drive north, my memories, finally unlocked, vied for attention. White-knuckled rides with Pooz at the wheel, her foot even heavier than mine. Our collaboration on a business book back in her days at a consulting firm, the two of us laughing raucously about her company's impenetrable jargon. Our secret language: her roll of the eyes in answer to my roll of the eyes at something Mom had said. Each of these were small moments, sister moments. Nothing I wanted to share. I was relieved that Jonathan once again would be speaking for the Smolowes. As for the other scheduled speakers, I was anticipating a feeling of uplift from their stories and a sense of bittersweet happiness at hearing my sister celebrated.

The event was, without doubt, a very Poozian affair. The location, a large grassy quadrangle on the Dartmouth campus encircled by sheltering trees, spoke to Ann's love of the outdoors and her love of her alma mater (which showed its love for her by lowering the campus's college flags to half-mast). The speakers, who traversed her work, social, and family spheres, told wonderful stories that showcased Ann's derring-do spirit, her humor and ability to laugh at herself, her strong sense of mentorship, friendship, and kinship. It was impossible not to laugh as college friends recounted some of her more ridiculous youthful escapades. (One speaker devilishly wielded a toilet plunger to illustrate her story.) And it was impossible not to cry as colleagues evoked Ann's giving nature. Yes, there was plenty of uplift. Though Ann had died way too soon, she'd packed a lot of living into her fifty-one years.

Yet it isn't the remembrances that have stayed with me. Instead, what lingers and provides comfort stems from something that occurred to me later: not once during those eulogies did I silently cry out, *Where are you, Pooz? You should be hearing this.* I didn't have to. As I sat there laughing and crying, I knew I was hearing nothing that Ann hadn't heard, too. When friends, relatives, and colleagues had descended on her home to say their good-byes, they'd shared their memories, thanks, and love with Ann in the here and now—rather than saving them for a congregation of mourners in the there and later. Each of them had done what my friend Richard had suggested after Joe's diagnosis: they'd assumed the worst and poured their hearts out.

Ann, in effect, had gotten to attend her own memorial service. She died knowing what she meant to the people who'd made her life so rich; what impact she'd had on each of them; what they found humorous about her; what they admired, valued, and loved most about her; why they would miss her; why she would always remain a part of their lives. Before Ann closed her eyes for the last time, she'd been able to see the depth of the heart print she would leave behind.

I can think of no better good-bye for those who are departing.

I can think of no better good-bye for those who will remain.

EPILOGUE

Dᴜʀɪɴɢ ᴛʜᴇ ғɪʀsᴛ ʏᴇᴀʀ ᴏғ ᴡɪᴅᴏᴡʜᴏᴏᴅ, my main challenge had been to figure out how to keep going with a huge hole in the center of my being. Joe was such a raw absence that he remained a constant presence. That changed in year two. No longer awaking to thoughts of Joe every morning and no longer falling asleep to thoughts of him every night, I felt his three-dimensionality flattening. My memories began to seem more like vacation photos than the experience itself. As Wease grew a little less vivid with each passing day, I felt like I was losing him all over again—this time irretrievably. Heartsick, I wondered if this dimming was what widowed people meant when they said, "The second year is harder than the first." Then in year three, memories of Joe and the pain of his absence began to resurge with increasing vividness.

The ache started after Becky received her first college acceptance letter late in the fall of 2011. Bob had accompanied us on most of our campus tours, nearly a dozen in all. Yet as Becky and I jumped up and down, shrieking like two little kids, Joe was the man with whom I shared the moment. *Can you believe this, Wease?* I marveled silently. *Our baby is going to college!*

Six months later, Bob was again the man at my side, Joe the one on my mind, as I sat at the crew team's spring awards banquet. Becky had been an indifferent athlete through her elementary and middle school years. She'd grumbled through swim instruction; hung up her soccer shoes after two seasons; played softball without distinction, one of those kids with mediocre hand-eye coordination and wandering attention who, consigned to the outfield, could be counted on only some of the time to get the job done. Joe and I had been delighted, but surprised, when she announced her freshman year of high school that she wanted to row. Crew is a grueling sport. And the coaches, an attractive married couple, both once members of the British national team, were not the coddling sort. At their first meeting with parents, they told us, "The only excuse for your child to miss a practice is if there's a death in the family." They weren't kidding. Joe and I figured that between the missed spring vacations and 4:00 a.m. wake-up calls for weekend regattas, Becky's enthusiasm would wane quickly.

We figured wrong. Each winter as she endured brutal indoor training, the boring workouts on erg machines rippling her body with rock-hard muscles, Becky proved to be her father's daughter: a completist, not a complainer. She never let on if it stung that Joe hadn't witnessed her evolution into a deeply committed and highly focused competitor. Instead, each spring, Bob's was the male voice cheering her from the banks of the Schuylkill and Cooper Rivers as she racked up city, state, and national medals.

Yet on this night, when the coaches handed Becky her varsity letter, the impact of Joe not being there to share in her achievement walloped me. *Isn't this incredible, Wease? Our daughter. A varsity letter. Who would have thought?*

Three weeks later when senior prom night rolled around, Lynn and I sat talking on my back porch while Becky dressed. Seemingly out of nowhere, Lynn asked, "How *are* you?"

"I'm sorry?"

"You know. Tomorrow."

Tomorrow? It took me a moment to realize Lynn was referring

to the three-year anniversary of Joe's death. "I'm fine," I said. "I know it's coming."

Lynn's expression—part sympathy, part skepticism—suggested she didn't quite believe me. So, I told her about Bob's experience on the first anniversary of his wife's death. He'd shown up at my house that evening uncharacteristically irritable after receiving an e-mail from his brother-in-law that said he was thinking of Bob on this difficult day. Bob understood his brother-in-law was trying to be sensitive about a day he assumed would distress Bob. But Bob hadn't been distressed; after anticipating the anniversary for weeks, the actual occasion had slipped by him. He didn't appreciate the reminder.

"What people don't understand," I said to Lynn, "is that Leslie is with Bob all the time, just as Joe is with me all the time. For predictable occasions like anniversaries and holidays, you begin girding weeks in advance, so they usually aren't the ones that hurt. It stings much more when something blindsides you."

Suddenly, the kitchen door swung open and Becky stepped onto the porch decked out for prom: a short beige dress fitted tight across the bodice and poufy at the bottom; four-inch-high heels; artfully applied makeup; hair swept up and lined with a marvel of thin braids. Though I'm well acquainted with my daughter's physical attributes and distinctive sense of style, her beauty literally took my breath away. Lynn gasped, too.

Look at her, Wease. She's absolutely stunning.

As I blinked back tears, I murmured to Lynn, "This is what I mean about being blindsided. Joe should be here to see this."

The next evening, June 20, marked the anniversary of Joe's death. When Becky and I made our annual visit to the cemetery, both of us were dry-eyed as we sat beside his headstone, unmoved by either the place or the occasion. Coming at the end of a long day of shopping to equip Becky for her summer job as a camp counselor, the visit felt like one more errand to be checked off our to-do list. We agreed that feelings of missing Dad couldn't be summoned by the calendar. They came when they came.

"Still," I said, "certain occasions are bound to hurt, like tomorrow, when he won't be there to see you get your high school diploma. He would have been so proud of you."

"Do you really think so?" Becky asked.

"God, yes," I said, my eyes no longer dry.

Graduation day dawned blisteringly hot, and though the mercury kept climbing, Bob, Gay, and I showed up early to secure places together in the outdoor amphitheater, where the tiers of large rocks that serve as bleachers were certain to fill quickly. I thought I'd come fully armed: a cushion to sit on; an icepack to press between my thighs; a pack of Kleenex to mop my predictable, sappy tears. But I'd come undefended against the sight of so many intact sets of parents, many of whom I hadn't encountered since Becky's primary school years when Joe had been at my side for the school plays and backyard birthday parties. Time had left its mark, etching not only lines into the couple's faces, but a deeper two-ness into their interactions. Watching them confer with such comfortable familiarity, I felt Joe's absence gnaw.

I was still holding it together as the first waves of graduates poured across two stone bridges to take seats facing their parents. When I spotted Becky, mid-bridge, in her royal blue cap and gown, I thought, *There she is, Wease.* That's when I lost it. Tears of pride and joy. Tears of sadness and loss. Tears of This-is-so-wrong-you're-not-here-to-see-this. Way too many tears for one small packet of Kleenex. *Where are you, Wease?* I thought as I lowered my sunglasses.

That longing grew more intense over the next week as Bob, Becky, and I toured the charming towns and cities of southern Spain. For months, Becky and I had been looking forward to this trip, a long-promised graduation hurrah. I'd asked her godfathers, their two daughters, and our friends Paige and Phil to join us, knowing that without Joe's infallible sense of direction to guide, I would get hopelessly lost in the Andalusian mountains. Ken, in turn, had invited his parents. Some part of my brain understood what was shaping up, but it didn't hit me until we were all assembled at the house Arthur had rented: Bob apart, these were the same people Joe and I had looked forward to sharing a house with in Tuscany in 2008 before an emergency hospitalization scuttled our plans. Now, I felt Joe's absence deepen with each passing day.

On our last evening together before Becky and I headed on to Bruges and Amsterdam, Paige said to me, "We've all been saying how we much miss Joe."

Unexpectedly, I felt a surge of irritation. They'd been talking about Joe and hadn't thought to include me in the conversation? "I miss Joe, too," I said with more vehemence than I intended. "Nobody talks to me about Joe. I wish they would."

Both parts of that statement were true. The silence I'd found so bewildering during my free-range shiva had never eased. Three years on, even casual references to Joe—something he'd liked or said or done—were still so rare that I almost never heard his name, except from Bob. For us, references to Joe and Leslie remained a routine part of our dialogue. But talking about Wease with Bob was satisfying only up to a point. Bob, after all, never knew Joe.

I returned from the trip feeling frustrated. Lynn's concern about the impact of Joe's third anniversary hadn't sat right. My Pennsylvania friends' hesitation to talk about Joe in front of me hadn't sat right either. "It's amazing," Lynn said. "Three years later, you're still dealing with people's preconceptions about death."

After my acute yearning for Joe subsided and I reflected on Lynn's observation, I realized that I, too, continue to suffer from preconceptions. Glad to be relieved of That Woman status and restored to full personhood, I assumed my friends had no further role to play as I dealt with the gradually changing nature of my grief. I also assumed people's continuing reluctance to mention Joe in front of me stemmed from the same misplaced concern I'd sensed at the shiva, namely that any reference to him might upset me. But people's reticence, I now learned, was more complicated. Lynn observed that because I hadn't welcomed talk of Joe when he was sick, some people perhaps assumed that I still preferred not to talk about him. Paige told me that during the Spain trip, people had felt awkward talking about Joe in front of Bob.

Of course they did. How could these friends know that Bob and I sprinkle our conversation liberally with references to our deceased spouses? How could they know that far from bringing me down, mentions of Joe give me a lift? How could they know that their well-intended *omertà* surrounding all-things-Joe makes me feel at times not only that Joe has been forgotten, but also that he and I have been erased as a couple? All of this reminded me of the crucial lesson Ann had offered back at the start of Joe's illness: "I can't know what you need unless you tell me."

It also reminded me of the widow who, a year past her husband's death, told me, "People act as if he never existed." Her solution had been to dine exclusively with the two couples who kept her husband in the conversation. My own remedy has been to tell friends that I'd prefer they not censor spontaneous memories or mentions of Joe for fear of upsetting me. His death hasn't diminished the significance of the twenty-seven years we spent together. I love hearing about him; I love remembering those years. It's been a slow trajectory, digging out from under the images of Joe in sickness, then in death, to recapture vivid memories of happier times when our loving and cherishing was also blessed by good health. Other people's verbal snapshots help.

I've had an easier time retrieving images of my sister and my mother in happier, healthier times, maybe because I've had more opportunity to share memories. One or the other often arises in my conversations with my father, my brothers, Gatha, or Jim (who's now engaged to Patsy). Perhaps this hunger we all share to restore Mom and Ann to vitality in our memories is part of what was meant by the two widowed people who told me, "It takes five years to get over your grief."

I try not to anticipate. Best, I feel, to let grief guide where it may. Right now, I'm heartened by my recent flare-up of longing for Joe. Though it hurt to again be missing him so intensely, it was also reassuring. I haven't lost Wease irretrievably. He is still with me.

I hope he'll continue to be with me when Bob moves in after Becky leaves for college a few weeks from now. That's a lot of change to absorb. But, inevitably, life goes on.

So does sickness and dying. Two recent magazine cover stories, one in *Time*, the other in *New York*, about Baby Boomers dealing with the challenges of their aging parents' fragile health signal that Boomers are beginning to rethink what they want for their parents—and, by extension, for themselves—as they consider a person's twilight years. Is life at any cost really worth the price, literally and figuratively? Should there be a limit to suffering? Who makes that call? And how do you make that call without guilt? Lynn, whose mother-in-law is suffering from advanced Alzheimer's, told me recently, "You just got there sooner than the rest of us."

While I still find no meaning in Joe's death, I, like my friend Richard, find great meaning in sharing what I've learned, if it can be of use to someone. I no longer shy from people's pain, tongue-tied. I also no longer extend vague offers of "anything." When a neighbor's father died recently, I offered rooms in my house to accommodate relatives descending for the memorial service. When a former neighbor I don't know well lost her husband suddenly, I paid a condolence call, a copy of Bonanno's book in hand. When I learned a college friend whom I hadn't seen in decades was about to see her husband through a stem cell transplant, I got in touch to ask if she'd have use for some caregiving tips I'd learned during Joe's transplant.

In each case, I strove to let the other person's signals guide. With my neighbor, I wound up hosting four of her family members. After one visit with the widow, I bowed out, sensing she had a strong support network and wasn't looking to enlarge it. With my college friend, I remained in touch until her husband was on the mend, offering encouragement through the grueling days of cell destruction, then tips for insuring a germ-free homecoming. At no point during those months did I mention that Joe had died. When we finally got together, her first words were, "I didn't know about Joe! Why didn't you tell me?"

"Because you didn't need me to put that thought in your head," I said. "Your imagination could go there all by itself."

For a moment, her shoulders sagged. "Yeah. It could."

If I sound like I know what I'm doing, please don't be fooled. Lynn says I have "a PhD in death and dying," and she's not wrong to suggest circumstance has made me knowledgeable about navigating caregiving and grief. But what I know more certainly than anything else is this: my trove of information is a perfect fit for one person only—me. As a result, I feel hardly more self-assured today dealing with people's pain and stress than I did that long ago day in the parking lot when I spotted Elizabeth. Then, I felt I knew too little to make the "right" move. Today, I feel at risk of downloading more information than might be welcome or useful. Either way, both draw on my projections of what the other person must be feeling and needing. I've learned how unhelpful *that* can be.

These days, I'm struggling to find the right balance with my friend Callie, who recently began aggressive treatment for breast cancer. When news of Callie's diagnosis first reached me, it hit with a force beyond my understandable concern for a friend facing hideous amounts of chemo, radiation, and surgery. It took me a few days to realize I was reacting not only to the ordeal Callie was about to undergo, but to the ordeal her husband, Don, was about to endure, as well. Though I know Don only socially, something about him and Callie as a couple, their connectedness, the delight they take in one another, reminds me of Joe and me. So after reaching out to Callie, I also made an overture to Don via e-mail, alert to the possibility that I might make him as uncomfortable as my colleague had made me, back when I feared her widowhood might be contagious. The one time I've sat down with both Callie and Don, I shared a few thoughts they seemed to find helpful; I also shared a few thoughts that later made me cringe, thinking I may have overshot the mark. Probably more useful, while they were away on vacation, I noticed a pile-up of mail and packages on their front doorstep. I sent Callie an e-mail asking if she'd like me to take in the stack and got a grateful reply. Sometimes, it's just that easy.

Recently, Callie talked with me about some of the draining aspects of her evolving situation. Her list included repetitive and overly prying questions. Expressions of concern that felt more like demands for reassurance than genuine offers of support. Vague offers of "anything" that resonated in her ear as "nothing." I recognize that script. I'm trying to steer clear of it. I'm also trying, given my own experience, to check whatever assumptions I may have at the door. This is about Callie, not me.

Inescapably, in coming years it will be about more and more

of my friends. As sickness and caregiving, death and grief become increasingly familiar to all of us, I don't expect that my desire to offer help and support will diminish. I also don't expect that accumulating experience with life's most painful situations will prepare me to approach any one friend's heartache with greater confidence. I have a deep appreciation for just how individual and unpredictable feelings and needs can be.

Life, too. When Joe was first diagnosed in 2007, I thought that if I lost him I would have to reimagine my life because the one I had would no longer be one I'd want to inhabit. Five years, four deaths, and many hard-earned lessons later, I feel much as I felt during my happy decades with Joe: very fortunate to have the life I have. There are huge holes in its fabric, but I neither expect nor want them to mend. Instead, I ride out the moments when I feel my most rewarding days are behind; and I seize the moments when I feel my most rewarding days still lie ahead.

Weasel Update: I'm okay. I really am.

—August 2012

POSTSCRIPT

Six weeks after I finished writing this book, Bob and I became engaged. As friends and family showered us with excited congratulations, I felt their excitement was greater than ours. Though we'd been together only two and a half years, Bob and I had already been through so much together. On my side, there had been the death of my sister, the death of my mother, and my daughter's departure for college. On his side, there had been the death of his mother and the loss of two jobs, each vaporized by the bleak economy. All of this had eliminated the guesswork about whether we'd be there for each other "for better, for worse, for richer, for poorer." Our histories with Joe and Leslie had similarly removed the mystery about "in sickness and in health." Bob and I loved each other. We couldn't imagine going forward without each other. To us, marriage was simply the next step.

But while both of us wanted to *be* married, neither of us much wanted to *get* married. We'd each done the tux-and-gown thing before. Bob's first wedding, with its two hundred guests, had been an extravagant dream—his in-laws'. Mine, with a crowd of one hundred, had involved enough family soapsuds to last a lifetime. In recent years, Bob had culled the ties from his wardrobe, I the heels and stockings from mine. The idea of eloping held appeal.

Then we got real. Foremost, there were our children to consider. While we couldn't know if any of them would have been just as glad not to attend, we didn't want to risk any of them feeling left out. Also, it was important to us that Becky, Bex, and Adam witness our ceremony. While Bob and I had no illusions that the five us would ever be the Brady Bunch, our marriage would affect all of us. Our kids deserved—no, they needed—to be there. Besides, I couldn't imagine taking such a life-changing step without Becky present.

There were a handful of others we felt should be there, too: my father (the sole remaining parent between us), Bob's two brothers, my two brothers, Gatha (my stand-in mom), and Lynn (my stand-in sister). As for our friends, in-laws, and extended family, we could only hope they would understand our desire to keep the wedding small. It wasn't only that neither of us wanted to plan or be the focus of a lavish affair. Neither of us wanted to feel like we were dancing on the graves of the two people whose deaths had given rise to this occasion. Joe was still Becky's dad; Leslie was still Bex and Adam's mom. We wanted to be respectful of that—and of our cherished late spouses, who Bob and I knew would very much be with us as we exchanged vows.

Things fell into place with remarkable ease. With our guests spread out along the East Coast from New York to Florida, we decided that my dad's retirement village in North Carolina would be a convenient midway point. The village's administrative staff agreed to reserve suites for our guests and the private dining room for our wedding dinner; the kitchen staff agreed to prepare the meal and the cake; my mother's favorite local florist agreed to provide a bouquet and decorative arrangements. Fuss factor? Zero.

As for the ceremony, those details fell into place, too. While scouting the village's public rooms (all of which felt too cavernous for our small crowd), my eyes were drawn to a tall, wide window on the open floor above the main living room. When I wandered up, I discovered that the floor-to-ceiling window was bordered on each side by enough wall to create the feeling of a cozy alcove. Perfect! Flank the window with two tall end tables, top each one with a flower arrangement, and voila: instant chapel.

Best of all, Bex, who's an ordained minister with the online Universal Life Church, agreed to conduct the wedding service; Becky agreed to be my maid of honor; Adam agreed to be Bob's best man. The pieces were all in place.

On January 19, 2013, surrounded by our children, Bob and I married.

—May 2013

ACKNOWLEDGMENTS

My THANKS TO:

Lisa Gornick, Jillian Medoff, Paula Span, and Nancy Star for their thoughtful comments and astute suggestions;

Phyllis Heller, Marion Roach Smith, and Margot Sage-EL for their vision and counsel;

The Smolowe men, Dick, Alan, and Jonathan, for their insights and encouragement;

Gail Hochman, agent extraordinaire, for her energy and support;

Brooke Warner, for her enthusiasm and guidance;

Becky Treen, for her patience and inspiration;

Bob Schwartz, for his understanding and love each day, every day.

ABOUT THE AUTHOR

photo © Esme

Jᴉʟʟ Sᴍᴏʟᴏᴡᴇ is the author of the memoir *An Empty Lap: One Couple's Journey to Parenthood* and co-editor of the anthology *A Love Like No Other: Stories from Adoptive Parents*. An award-winning journalist, she has been a foreign affairs writer for *Time* and *Newsweek*, and a senior writer for *People*, where she currently specializes in crime stories. Her articles and essays have appeared in many publications and anthologies, including the *New York Times*, the *Boston Globe*, *The Washington Post Magazine*, *More*, *Adoptive Families* and the *Reader's Digest* "Today's Best NonFiction" series. In her work as a grief and transition coach, she partners with clients to help them identify—then take—the steps that will restore momentum to their lives.

She can be reached at jillsmolowe@gmail.com and through her website, www.jillsmolowe.com.

SELECTED TITLES FROM SHE WRITES PRESS

She Writes Press is an independent publishing company founded to serve women writers everywhere. Visit us at www.shewritespress.com.

Splitting the Difference: A Heart-Shaped Memoir by Tré Miller-Rodríguez $19.95, 978-1-938314-20-9
When 34-year-old Tré Miller-Rodríguez's husband dies suddenly from a heart attack, her grief sends her on an unexpected journey that culminates in a reunion with the biological daughter she gave up at 18.

Breathe: A Memoir of Motherhood, Death, and Family Conflict by Kelly Kittel $16.95, 978-1-938314-78-0
A mother's heartbreaking account of losing two sons in the span of nine months—and learning, despite all the obstacles in her way, to find joy in life again.

Three Minus One: Stories of Parents' Love and Loss edited by Sean Hanish and Brooke Warner $17.95, 978-1-938314-80-3
A collection of stories and artwork by parents who have suffered child loss that offers insight into this unique and devastating experience.

Warrior Mother: A Memoir of Fierce Love, Unbearable Loss, and Rituals that Heal by Sheila K. Collins, PhD $16.95, 978-1-938314-46-9
The story of the lengths one mother goes to when two of her three adult children are diagnosed with potentially terminal diseases.

Loveyoubye: A Memoir of Betrayal by Rossandra White $16.95, 978-1-938314-50-6
A soul-searching memoir detailing the painful, but ultimately liberating, disintegration of a twenty-five-year marriage.

Letting Go into Perfect Love: Discovering the Extraordinary After Abuse by Gwendolyn M. Plano $16.95, 978-1-938314-74-2
After staying in an abusive marriage for twenty-five years, Gwen Plano finally broke free—and started down the long road toward healing.

CPSIA information can be obtained at www.ICGtesting.com
Printed in the USA
BVOW04s1130240414

351606BV00005B/142/P